Congo Square in New Orleans

by
Jerah Johnson
The University of New Orleans

The Samuel Wilson, Jr. Publications Fund
of the
Louisiana Landmarks Society

Reprinted by permission of the Louisiana Historical Association
and the author, from **Louisiana History** (Spring, 1991),
117-157, where it originally appeared under the title
"New Orleans's Congo Square:
An Urban Setting for Early Afro-American Culture Formation."
Illustrations of drawings by Benjamin Henry Latrobe
and of engravings by E.W. Kemble have been added,
with commentary on these by John Joyce,
Tulane University, and Jerah Johnson

Library of Congress Catalog Number 95-80469
ISBN 1-879714-06-X

Second Printing, 2000

Cover: An 1885 engraving of a New Orleans "Congo Woman"
by E.W. Kemble.
See comment on the illustrations of Kemble.

New Orleans's Congo Square

By JERAH JOHNSON

University of New Orleans

Shortly after he completed repairs on the national capitol, which the British had burned when they captured Washington during the War of 1812, Benjamin Henry Latrobe proceeded to New Orleans. There he was to oversee construction of the waterworks he had designed for the century-old French city, recently acquired by the United States as part of the massive Louisiana Purchase. As the *Clio*, on which he had sailed from Baltimore, pulled up to the New Orleans wharves in early January of 1819, "everything," Latrobe wrote in his journal, "had an *odd* look." It was impossible, he continued, "not to stare at a sight wholly new even to one who has travelled much in Europe & America."

Curious market boats, "differing in form & equipment from anything that floats on the Atlantic side of our country," laden with exotic foodstuffs and some still flying the French tricolor, crowded the docks. And on the levee, "as far as the eye could reach" in either direction, "ranged two rows of market people, some having stalls or tables with a tilt or awning of canvas, but the majority having their wares lying on the ground, perhaps on a piece of canvas, or a parcel of Palmetto leaves." Five hundred or more "white men and women, & of all hues of brown, & of all classes of faces, from round Yankees, to grisly & lean Spaniards, black negroes and negresses, filthy Indians half naked, mulattoes, curly & straight-haired, quarteroons of all shades, long haired & frizzled, the women dressed in the most flaring yellow & scarlet gowns, the men capped and hatted" bought and sold "wild ducks, oysters, poultry of all kinds . . . bananas, piles of oranges, sugar cane, sweet & Irish potatoes, corn in the Ear & husked, apples, carrots & all sorts of other roots, eggs, trinkets, tin ware, dry goods . . . wretched beef . . . & some excellent & large fish," as well as a few books in English and French. All in all, he said, "more & odder things" than he could count.

On Sunday afternoon a fortnight or so later, while exploring the "back-of-town" of the city, away from the river, Latrobe heard in the distance an extraordinary noise, which he "supposed to proceed from some horse mill, the horses trampling on a wooden floor." But he found, as he approached, the sound to be "5 or 600 persons assembled in an open space or public square." All those "engaged in the business seemed to be *blacks*," for he "did not observe a dozen yellow faces" in the crowd. The crowd he discovered, when he moved into it to see what was going on, comprised not a single mass, but a series of clusters. The members of each cluster crowded around to form a rough circle, "the largest not ten feet in diameter." In the middle or on the edge of each circle sat or squatted two or three musicians, and, in most circles, around or in front of the musicians, from two to a dozen dancers moved to the rhythm of the circle's music, song, and chant.

The thunderous din that Latrobe had mistaken for the thumping of horse hooves came from the echoes of percussions of hundreds of hands and sticks on drums, gourds, and hollow, cotter-shaped, wooden blocks, all backed by the plunking of a variety of banjo-like instruments made from calabashes affixed to long fingerboards. In one circle Latrobe saw two women dancers holding "a coarse handkerchief extended by the corners in their hands" and gravely treading a "dull & slow figure, hardly moving their feet or bodies." In another, particularly large, circle, "a dozen women walked, by way of dancing, round the music in the center," and chanted, or "squalled out," as he said, a monotonous two-note refrain. In yet another group a man sang "an uncouth song to the dancing which I suppose was in some African language, for it was not French, and the women screamed a detestable burthen on one single note." "Never," Latrobe said, had he "seen anything more brutally savage." These Sunday amusements, he concluded, "have perpetuated here those of Africa among its inhabitants."[1]

Benjamin Latrobe had stumbled into New Orleans's old *Place des Nègres,* better known for most of its history as Congo Square. And from his time to ours, observers and scholars, particularly music history scholars, have continued to describe and analyze the beat of the *bamboulas,* the wail of the *banzas,* and the congeries of African dances that became the hallmark of the square. No other single spot has been more often mentioned in scholarly speculations about the origins of jazz or about the relationship of pre-jazz New Orleans music to jazz itself.[2] One reason for such attention has been that, unlike other, fly-by-night pre-jazz and early jazz settings—the countless black-town kitchens, garages, backyards, barrooms, and nightclubs in New Orleans, St. Louis, Kansas City, Chicago,

[1]Benjamin Henry Latrobe, *Impressions Respecting New Orleans: Diary and Sketches, 1818-1820,* ed. by Samuel Wilson, Jr. (New York, 1951), pp. 21-25, 49-51. Included in this edition are some remarkable sketches Latrobe made of the market vendors as well as the African musical instruments he saw in Congo Square. The time of day Latrobe saw the square, early afternoon, accounts for his seeing only very slow dancing. He had set out to walk with a friend from the turning basin of the Carondelet Canal, which was adjacent to the square, along the canal bank to Bayou St. John and back, two-and-a-half miles. Had he gone into the square at a later hour, say on his return trip—which he did not, but only noted that "returning after sunset near the same spot, the noise was still heard"—he would have witnessed the frenzied phase of the dances described by other observers.

[2]See, for example, the standards: Frederic Ramsey, Jr., and Charles E. Smith, eds., *Jazzmen* (New York, 1939); Robert Goffin, et al., *Jazz: From the Congo to the Metropolitan* (New York, 1944); Rudi Blesh, *Shining Trumpets: A History of Jazz,* 2 vols., rev. ed. (New York, 1958); Rex Harris, *Jazz,* 4th ed., rev. ed. (1946; reprint ed., London, 1956); Barry Ulanov, *A History of Jazz in America* (New York, 1952); Marshall W. Stearns, *The Story of Jazz* (New York, 1956); Henry A. Kmen, *Music in New Orleans: The Formative Years, 1791-1841* (Baton Rouge, 1966); Martin T. Williams, *Jazz Masters in New Orleans* (New York, 1967); Gunther Schuller, *Early Jazz: Its Roots and Musical Development* (New York, 1968); Frank Tirro, *Jazz: A History* (New York, 1977); Leroy Ostransky, *Jazz City: The Impact of Our Cities on the Development of Jazz* (Englewood Cliffs, N.J., 1978). Henry Kmen, "The Roots of Jazz and the Dance in Place Congo: A Re-Appraisal," *Inter-American Musical Research Yearbook,* VIII (1972), 5-17, corrects many of their errors but makes some of his own, particularly on the dating of the last African or Afro-American dances in Congo Place. See below, note 47. The precise relationship of jazz, which came out of New Orleans's English-speaking community, to the classical, *i. e.,* literate, musical tradition of the city's black Creole community remains yet to be fully explored by music historians.

and Harlem—the square has had a continuous history, and one that is largely documentable.

Taking account not only of the musical aspects of the square but of a number of non-musical aspects of its history gives Congo Square a special importance. The music-making in the square came to rival the highly romanticized "Quadroon Balls" as antebellum New Orleans's most celebrated public black institution. And at the same time the square's activities constituted, in a larger sense, a citywide institution that involved, in one way or another, and for over a century, a large number of New Orleanians, black and white. As Arlin Turner said in his prizewinning study of George W. Cable: "No spot in New Orleans could better . . . suggest the history of the lower half of the population, and through contrasts the upper half as well."[3]

When its unusual origins and a life span far longer than hitherto supposed are taken into account, Congo Square becomes uniquely significant. Its story not only bears upon the development of jazz and the history of black New Orleans, but adds to our understanding of the physical growth of the early city, its economic development, and the formation of its social and ethnic configuration, as well as the evolution of its celebrated public culture. And perhaps most importantly, it identifies a point of origin, indeed probably the major point of origin, of modern American dance.

Congo Square, nestled at the foot of the towering facade of the New Orleans Municipal Auditorium on Rampart Street and surrounded by a high new fence with a locked gate, looks today more like the landscaped frontage of a public building than it does a public square. Only its eighteen large live oaks hint at its age. And even those are young compared to their setting. They were planted in 1893 when the city fathers, in an ironic move, renamed the square in honor of former Confederate General P. G. T. Beauregard, who had just died. For most of its history before that time the square had been simply an open, grass-covered field with only a few trees. It always remained different from New Orleans's other squares because it was never really laid out by the city's planners as a public square. Instead it took its shape gradually and informally out of

[3]*George W. Cable: A Biography* (Baton Rouge, 1966), p. 229.

peculiarly New Orleanian circumstances. It was, in its origins as in its development, always of the people, an aspect of its character that was recognized when the spot was, for a brief time after the American purchase, officially designated *La Place Publique*.

Congo Square, however, originated not in the early American decades of New Orleans's history, but nearly a hundred years before, in the early decades of its French colonial period, and not as a spot where black New Orleanians gathered to dance, play, and sing, but as one of the city's public markets. The famous dancing, playing, and singing represented by-products of the square's market function.

For twenty years or more after its founding in 1699, France's Louisiana colony regularly faced the threat of starvation. During its first decade, the colony, lacking local production and perpetually short of imported foodstuffs, became entirely dependent upon nearby Indians for sustenance. But what the Indians could supply barely supported the local garrisons, leaving nothing for newly arriving colonists. Consequently, the newcomers often had to be dispersed, sometimes for long periods, to live with Indian tribes until a place could be found for them. At least four times between 1703 and 1710 food supplies completely ran out, and even the garrison troops had to abandon the settlements and take refuge for weeks or months with the Indians.[4]

During the second decade the situation briefly improved, only to worsen again suddenly. The complications following the collapse and reorganization of the Company of the Indies in 1721, the second of the two proprietaries that held the colony between 1712 and 1731, cut off not only food imports but virtually all capital supplies. Hard-pressed planters banked upon expansion of their slave-labor forces to save them. However, during the lag time between such expansion and net profits from it, they found themselves near penniless. In many cases they could not even afford to feed their increased number of slaves.

[4]Marcel Giraud, *Histoire de la Louisiane française*, 5 vols. (Paris, 1953-1990), I, 130-154, 162-179, 205-226, 235-266. Volume I of Giraud's series was translated into English, by Joseph C. Lambert as *A History of French Louisiana, 1698-1715* (Baton Rouge, 1974), the pagination of which is slightly different from the French original. See pages 141-167, 175-194, 225-245, 256-289.

To solve the problem, the planters moved to make their slaves more nearly self-sufficient. They began to assign slaves individual parcels of land on which to grow their own food as well as sale crops.[5]

Moreover, the planters began to see advantages for themselves in abiding by article five of the *Code Noir*, a provision thitherto honored more in its breach than in its observance. That article exempted slaves from forced labor on Sundays and religious holidays. On those "free days," which shortly came to include Saturday afternoons as well, slaves began to hire themselves out for wages or take their surplus products—not only foodstuffs and cash crops they had grown on their plots, but also gleanings of nuts and berries from the woods as well as fish and game from the swamps—into town and sell them, much as local Indians had been doing since the city was founded in 1718. And with the proceeds they could buy many of their own necessities, including articles of clothing.[6]

Jean-François Dumont, who came to New Orleans in 1719 from Quebec and in 1753 published his observations on the colony's early years, clearly documented the practice, which had become commonplace by the 1730s:

> Most of the slaves clear grounds and cultivate them on their own account, raising cotton, tobacco, &c. which they sell. Some [master's] give their negroes Saturday and Sunday to themselves, and during that time the master does not give them any food; they then work for other Frenchmen who have no slaves, and who pay them. Those who live in or near the capital

[5]Giraud, *Histoire de la Louisiane française*, II, 116-124, 129-146; III, 316-359; IV, 299-321; James T. McGowan, "The Creation of a Slave Society: Louisiana Plantations in the Eighteenth Century" (Ph. D. dissertation, University of Rochester, 1977), pp. 22-96. The first chapter of this dissertation appeared as "Planters Without Slaves: Origins of a New World Labor System," *Southern Studies*, XVI (1971), 5-26. McGowan's work, while it must be used with care because of some unsupported assertions and all too pat constructions, poses some important questions and offers some important insights that scholars of colonial Louisiana cannot afford to ignore.

[6]McGowan, "Creation of a Slave Society," pp. 135-145; Daniel H. Usner, "Frontier Exchange in the Lower Mississippi Valley: Race Relations and Economic Life in Colonial Louisiana, 1699-1783" (Ph. D. dissertation, Duke University, 1981), pp. 104-140.

> generally turn their two hours at noon to account by making faggots to sell in the city; others sell ashes, or fruits that are in season.[7]

Another French observer, Le Page Du Pratz, reflected in 1758 upon the sixteen years he had spent in the colony between 1718 and 1734. He ended his *History of Louisiana* with the admonition to masters that it was in "your own interest to give your negroes a small piece of waste ground . . . and to engage them to cultivate it for their own profit, that they may be able to dress a little better, by selling the produce. . . ." But, at the same time, he went on to warn that Sunday gatherings, particularly dances, could be the occasion for slaves' selling to one another stolen goods and also could be the occasion for plotting rebellions.[8]

Once established, the recognition of slaves' rights to free days, in the sense of enjoying the fruits of their own labor on such days, continued. Even during the 1740s, a decade during which planters enjoyed high demand and high prices for their indigo exports, the practice continued. On the contrary, one can judge the rapid growth as well as the rootedness of the practice from a celebrated court case. Though it occurred decades later, during the Spanish period, it furnished solid evidence of practices during the early French period.

The complex suit of *Charles Joseph Loppinot* v. *Jean Villeneuve* turned on two questions. How long had slaves' free days been recognized in the colony? And were masters required to give slaves written permission to work off their own plantations on such days? Villeneuve based his case on age-old recognition of free days without any necessity for written

[7]Jean-François-Benjamin Dumont de Montigny, *Mémoires historiques sur la Louisiane contenant ce qui y est arrivé de plus mémorable depuis l'année 1687, jusqu'à présent* . . ., 2 vols. (Paris, 1753), translated as "History of Louisiana" in Benjamin F. French, ed., *History of Louisiana*, 5 vols. (New York, 1846-1853), V, 120. The original manuscript of Dumont's work is in the Newberry Library in Chicago, signed only Lxxx Dxxx. Dumont, son of a Parisian lawyer, arrived in Louisiana after serving as a sublieutenant in the Quebec naval guard, stayed for over thirty years, returned to France 1747 and published his memoirs. The date of the above observation may be judged from context.

[8]Le Page du Pratz, *The History of Louisiana*, ed. by Joseph G. Tregle, Jr. (Baton Rouge, 1975), p. 387.

permissions; and Loppinot disputed both contentions. Each side called two planters as expert witnesses expected to support their respective claims. But to the consternation of Loppinot, all four experts, including his own, affirmed Villeneuve's position. The statements of one of them, the eighty-eight-year-old community patriarch, Pierre Delisle Dupard, cinched the argument. He testified that as far as he knew—and he was older than the colony itself—slaves' free days had been recognized without the necessity of formal written permission to work for others or themselves on those days. Such was the long-established "custom of the colony."[9]

There was, of course, nothing unique about Louisiana's slaves acting as merchants or being free to labor on Sundays. Slaves commonly did vending in South Carolina's low-country, for example, and the Sabbath was respected as a non-work day throughout the slaveholding American South. What made French Louisiana different was that slaves there came early to be recognized as having the right to use their free time virtually as they saw fit, with little or no supervision. Such a conception, much less such a practice, never prevailed anywhere in the rest of the South.

[9]The 1774 case was made complex because Villeneuve had made arrangements with Loppinot's slave, named Mulet, to build a chimney for him on one of his free Sundays. When the job was done, Villeneuve paid Mulet and as lagniappe gave him a bottle of brandy. On the way home, Mulet drank the bottle, got drunk, fell into a bayou, and drowned. Loppinot sued Villeneuve, demanding restitution for the property, Mulet, lost through Villeneuve's negligent and malfeasant action in giving him the brandy. But when the case came to hearing, Villeneuve's counselor, Leonard Mazange, argued that in such circumstances the rules of property law had no bearing. On his free days, he contended, Mulet, like all slaves, was, in terms of his labor, a free agent. And as such he had made and completed a work agreement. Hence, the case should be heard under the rules of contract. And, Mazange argued, while the *Code Noir* did not formally recognize free labor and called for written permissions from masters to sell anything, the old law of the colony, the ancient *Coutume de Paris*, accorded "customary local practice" precedence over statute or royal edict. The case was eventually appealed to Havana where the court ruled in Villeneuve's favor. Laura Porteous, trans., "Civil Procedures in Louisiana Under the Spanish Regime as Illustrated in Loppinot's Case, 1774," *Louisiana Historical Quarterly*, XII (1929), 49-120, provides a translation of the proceeding and Helen T. Catterall, *Judicial Cases Concerning American Slaves and the Negro*, Vol. III, *Cases from the Courts of Georgia, Florida, Alabama, and Louisiana* (Washington, D. C., 1932), pp. 429-430, summarizes the same document. McGowan, "Creation of a Slave Society," pp. 135-145, recounts the case in some detail. On the old law, see Jerah Johnson, "*La Coutume de Paris*: Louisiana's First Law," *Louisiana History*, XXX (1989), 145-155.

At first, and for quite a number of years, only a handful of slave peddlers occasionally sold goods up and down New Orleans's few short streets and along its riverfront, which served as the city's main food market.[10] The tiny town's population remained too small to have supported more. But as New Orleans's population grew, the vendors increased both their numbers and the regularity of their operations. In time, a number of slave merchants began to gather on Sundays at a certain spot and spread their wares on the open ground, thereby creating a regularly scheduled, stationary market of their own.

The market may have begun to take shape as early as the latter 1730s, but more likely in the late 1740s or the 1750s, by which time New Orleans's population approached the 2,000 mark. The 1730s and 1740s, which encompassed the ten-year-long terms of governors Jean-Baptiste de Bienville and the Marquis de Vaudreuil, saw both the city and the slave community stabilize. Previously New Orleans had been made up of a trickle of miscellaneous and largely transient troops and traders characteristic of frontier fortress towns. But by the 1740s, despite a continuing degree of rough social rowdiness, the city had developed a resident population sufficient to begin to jell as a little colonial society. Father Charles O'Neill termed those years "the classical period" of Louisiana's colonial history.[11]

Louisiana's slave population also underwent an unusual solidification process in the 1730s and 1740s. Virtually all slaves brought to Louisiana during the French period arrived in the nine-year period between 1722 and 1731. From the latter date to the end of the French period in 1763, only three hundred or so

[10]The riverfront served from the beginning, and well into the twentieth century, as the city's main food entrepot, and vestiges of that function remain even today in the form of a few remaining wholesale produce warehouses and the French Market.

[11]On the jelling of New Orleans' society in the 1730s and '40s, see Jerah Johnson, "Colonial New Orleans: A Fragment of the Eigtheenth-Century French Ethos," in Arnold Hirsch and Joseph Logsdon, eds., *Creole New Orleans: Race and Americanization* (Baton Rouge, forthcoming). Charles Edwards O'Neill's characterization occurs in his *Church and State in French Colonial Louisiana* (New Haven, Conn., 1966), p. 233. See also J. Zitomersky, "Urbanization in French Colonial Louisiana (1706-1766)," *Annales de démographie historique*, (1974), 263-278, a particularly interesting discussion of early Louisiana demography and geography.

additional slaves were imported. Moreover, as Gwendolyn Hall's recent work has shown, the overwhelming number of French colonial Louisiana slaves all came from a single region in Africa, the Senegal River basin, and brought with them an already formed and highly cohesive shared Bambara culture, a happenstance unique in the annals of slavery in the Americas. And among the notable attributes of Bambara culture was an established tradition of trade and city marketing. Indeed, the Bambara people were historically thought of as the preeminent "merchant princes" of the western Sudan.[12]

In addition to the indigenous tradition of marketing brought by Louisiana slaves from Africa, they found a model already in place in New Orleans in the form of the local Indian market. From the time Bienville founded New Orleans, a few Indians had brought fish, game, bear grease, medical and cooking herbs, baskets, and straw into town and sold them. But a larger number gathered and formed an Indian market a mile or so outside of the city, near where the Grand Route St. Jean, the main road north, encountered the Bayou St. Jean, which served as the major avenue for transport of goods into the city.[13]

The interaction of the Indian and African communities formed one of the most notable characteristics of New Orleans's

[12]Gwendolyn Midlo Hall, "The Formation of Creole Slave Culture During the Eigtheenth Century," in Hirsch and Logsdon, eds., *Creole New Orleans*. And on the Bambara trade, see Edward William Bovill, *The Golden Trade of the Moors* (London, 1958), which supersedes his earlier *Caravans of the Old Sahara*; and Florence Mahoney and H. D. Idwon, "The Peoples of Senegambia," in J. F. A. Ajayi and Ian Espie, *A Thousand Years of West African History*, rev. ed. (London, 1969), pp. 132-148. Maurice Delafosse's three-volume *Haut-Senegal-Niger* (Paris, 1912), is an old encyclopedic work on the area which is still useful, but should be complemented with more modern studies.

[13]Bayou St. John led, a few miles north of the city, into the vast lake system—Maurepas, Pontchartrain, and Borgne—that, in turn, opened directly into the Gulf of Mexico. That water route served as the main avenue for transport of goods into the city until the ever-shifting sandbars blocking entrance to the Mississippi River were brought under control by the channel and jetty system put in place by Captain James B. Eads in 1879. And even so, the lake-bayou route continued to furnish foodstuffs from the hinterlands until well after the turn of the century. The Indian market occupied an open area, that later became *Place Bretonne*, at the conjunction of what are now Esplanade Avenue, Bayou Road, Dorgenois, Bell, and DeSoto streets. The Municipal Market building, erected in 1867, still marks the spot, though the building now houses offices.

colonial history. Because most African slaves brought to Louisiana were males, great numbers married Indian women, whom the French colonials had early begun enslaving as food growers, cooks, bedfellows, and translators. Consequently, as the decades passed, there developed an unusually high degree of intermixing of the two groups and their cultures, an intermixing that, by the end of the nineteenth century, had resulted in the absorption of the local Indian populations into the New Orleans black community.[14]

The open ground upon which the slave vendors spread their wares and set up their market stalls stretched along the edge of the City Commons at the end of Orleans Street, just beyond where it abutted the low earthen breastworks and borrow pit that formed the city's limits and served as its primitive defense line. John Smith Kendall noted that the *Place des Nègres* lay in the "vicinity" of a spot which local Indians had long used for celebrating their annual corn feast or *fête du blé*.[15]

[14]On the Indian market and the relationship of the Indian and African communities, see Johnson, "Colonial New Orleans," and Hall, "Formation of Creole Slave Culture," as well as Usner, "Frontier Exchange." The present article develops the sketch of the Congo Square Market given in the first of these.

[15]George Washington Cable, "The Dance in Place Congo," *Century Magazine*, XXXI (February 1886), 518-519, placed the location on the edge of the Commons, "outside the rear gate, the poisonous wilderness on three sides." John Smith Kendall's mention occurred in his *History of New Orleans*, 3 vols. (New York, 1922), II, 679. He also noted that the Indian corn festival was commemorated in the first play written in Louisiana. He was referring to *La Fête du petit-blé, ou l'héroisme de Poucha-Houmma, tragédie en cinq actes; fait historique pris chez une nation sauvage* by Paul-Louis Leblanc de Villeneufve, a work that remains an important source of information on Choctaw life and customs. Villeneuve came to Louisiana in 1752 at the age of eighteen and served the colony for a number of years as a military officer, spending long periods living with the Indians. Later he lived in retirement in New Orleans, where he died in 1815. His play, which was first performed in Governor Louis Billouart de Kerlérec's residence in 1753, was published in 1814 by the *Courrier de la Nouvelle Orléans*, with a dedication to Madame de Laussat, wife of Louisiana's last French colonial prefect. It was reprinted in the *Comptes Rendus* of the New Orleans Athenée Louisianais (1909), 421-432, 443-464, 529-563; [1910], 13-30, 41-45. See Ruby Van Allen Caulfield, *The French Literature of Louisiana* (New York, 1929), pp. 6-7, 268-269. And on local Indians and on corn festivals, see Fred B. Kniffen, *et al.*, *The Historic Indian Tribes of Louisiana from 1542 to the Present* (Baton Rouge, 1987), pp. 50-51, 260-261, 273-274. See also, Le Page du Pratz, *History of Louisiana*, p. 311. Neither Cable nor Kendall indicate sources for their information. Presumably they gleaned it from older New Orleans residents. Cable, born in 1844, and Kendall, born in 1874, were both in positions to have gathered

At the time, the area of New Orleans adjacent to the City Commons comprised the "back-of-town" margin of the city. Although the streets on that side of town had been cut and their blocks platted, most of the lots stood vacant. Low-lying and waterlogged, that whole part of the city remained barely distinguishable from the sprawling *marais perdu* marsh and the wild commons across the breastwork mound. The only imposing installations in the isolated and desolate area were ones the city's inhabitants habitually shunned. St. John's "death house," a hospital for the destitute, blocked the end of Toulouse Street. And nearby in the Commons, on what would become the later extension of St. Peter Street, lay New Orleans's first cemetery.[16]

While the exact date of the market's formation in the 1740s or 1750s may have to remain a matter of conjecture, we can judge that by the last decade of French rule, the trading activities of slaves had come to form a significant feature of New Orleans's mercantile life, one sufficiently profitable to excite the attention, and envy, of local retail merchants. That is clear from a document that comes, again, from a somewhat later date but which tells us much about earlier practices. Two years after Spain took over administration of Louisiana in 1769, the local *procurador,* or attorney general, recommended to the *cabildo,* the city's governing council, that merchants be allowed, in spite of the law, to open their shops before and after divine services on

---

information from informants whose personal memories reached back to early American and late colonial times and whose living memories stretched back, through accounts they had heard as children from even older residents, into a quite early period. While such "saga history," as living memory is increasingly being called today, is highly susceptible to error, it usually contains at least a kernel of truth. In the present case, the independent information we have on the spatial development of early colonial New Orleans and on African-Indian relations makes Cable's location of the *Place des Negres* and Kendall's assertion of an Indian association not only plausible, but probable.

[16]Mary Louise Christovich, *et al., New Orleans Architecture,* vol. VI, Roulhac Toledano and Mary Louise Christovich, *Faubourg Tremé and the Bayou Road* (Gretna, La., 1980) has a useful sketch of Congo Square (pp. 63-66) and the City Commons (pp. 56-60). See also vol. III, Leonard Huber, *et al., The Cemeteries* (Gretna, La., 1974), pp. 1-3. The swampy City Commons, easily accessible over the breastwork which was so low as to be little more than a five-foot rise, was constantly used by the city's residents for hunting, trapping, fishing, gathering firewood, and pasturing animals.

Sundays in order to sell goods to slaves on their free days. It is clear from the wording of the petition that such slave buying power was not new but had been in existence for quite some time, well back into the 1760s, and probably into the 1750s.[17]

Throughout the French period the market activities of slaves remained in legal limbo. The *Code Noir* expressly forbade slaves to do any kind of work on Sundays and holy days, to own any kind of property, to conduct any kind of trade on their own account, to gather in large groups, or to hunt or sell goods, even for their masters, without written permission. On the other hand, the slave entrepreneurs provided much needed supplies to a city frequently, if not chronically, short of foodstuffs. The solution was for the authorities simply to do nothing and say nothing, and "assume" that the slave vendors were selling goods for their masters, and with permission. Hence the absence of any official mention of the market is not surprising.[18]

Even the periodic tightening of slave discipline affected the market little or not at all. For example, Governor Vaudreuil's famous move, in the 1750s, to bring a greater degree of social order to the still rowdy city seems to have left the market untouched. Appalled at the license and lack of decorum that characterized the local population, black and white, the "grand marquis," who, as the son of the governor of Canada, had grown up accustomed to a much more structured environment, issued in 1751 a "police code" for Louisiana's population, slave and free. While the long, thirty-article code detailed and outlawed

[17]The Spanish authorities, who effectively began establishing their administration in August 1769 with the arrival of General Alejandro O'Reilly and his army of occupation, spent the next few years evaluating elements of the established French practices and deciding which they would leave in place and which they would change. The deliberations referred to above were simply one example of that. In this case the new authorities decided not to interfere with the market practice. See WPA compilations of "Records and Deliberations of the Cabildo, 1769-1803," 15 vols., Louisiana Division, New Orleans Public Library, Petition of the Attorney General, January 10, 1771, I, 84-85. See also, McGowan, "Creation of a Slave Society," pp. 197-198.

[18]See especially articles 5, 12, 13, 15, and 22, of the *Code Noir*. Charles Gayarré included an English translation of the code, somewhat abridged, as an appendix to his *History of Louisiana*, 4 vols., 4th ed. (1903; reprint ed., New Orleans, 1965), I, 531-540. The full French text of the code appears in the *Louisiana Historical Society Publication*, IV (1908), 75-90.

an astonishing number of specific offenses being committed by slaves—as well as free people of color—absenteeism, stealing, prowling, unapproved visiting off plantations, selling goods without authorization, drinking, roaming the streets at night, dancing, plundering, assembling, carrying canes, rods or sticks, riding horses on roads and streets, and frequenting taverns and alehouses—it conspicuously made no mention of the market activities.

The specific prohibitions listed in the edict, when read in isolation, may appear to have affected the market. But when viewed in context, they are seen not to have been designed to do that at all. The prohibitions were aimed at marginal elements of the white population who were illegally catering to slaves, at crime control, particularly in the city, or at masters who were failing to properly control the behavior of slaves on their plantations. Vaudreuil laid no restrictions on the slave vendors or their Sunday market.[19]

In 1760, mid-way through the French and Indian War, the local military engineers strengthened New Orleans's defenses, a move that affected the market's physical relationship to the city. The engineers completely redesigned the simple, low, straight-line breastworks on the back-of-town side of the city. They moved the whole defense wall several hundred feet into the City Commons, dug a moat to replace the shallow old borrow pit, raised a much higher breastwork mound, and built a palisade wall atop it. In three places they jutted the new breastworks and wall outward to form sharp, triangular bastions. The one at the end of Orleans Street they named *Bastion Orléans*.

In the enlarged area within the city that resulted from moving the defense wall outward, the engineers extended the old short streets and cut a new long street, Rampart, along the line where the old breastworks had run. And in the remaining area they platted a new row of irregularly sized, trapezoidial blocks between the new street and the new wall. These were reserved for military purposes, but remained, for the rest of the French

[19]Gayarré appended a highly abridged translation of the police regulations to his *History of Louisiana*, II, 361-367. The full text appears in the Library of Congress microfilmed collection of materials from France's National Archives, Ministry of the Colonies, series C 13a, volume 35, folios 39ff. Many of the regulations simply echoed provisions of the *Code Noir*.

period, largely unused, wooded clumps. The thrusting out of the Orleans Bastion also brought within the city's walls the *Place des Nègres*. It remained open ground, lying across Rampart Street at the end of Orleans. There the slave merchants continued their market, on the very spot that, over half a century later, would come to be known as New Orleans's Congo Square.[20]

Three years after redesigning the city's defenses, France lost the seven-year long war with England, and with it, her entire North American empire. In 1763 England took Canada and Spain got France's vast Louisiana territories. The change of administration in New Orleans, finally effected only at the end of 1769, and the ensuing thirty-five years of Spanish rule saw the local slaves' market flourish. During that time New Orleans's economy improved dramatically, and its population jumped from less than 3,000 to more than 8,000. And the market grew apace.

All of Louisiana's French governors, save one, had come out of Canadian backgrounds, where African slavery was unknown. But the colony's Spanish governors all came to Louisiana from prior posts in Spain's New World empire, where African slavery was common. And, it is important to remember that Louisiana's Spanish governors served throughout the period under the direction of the captain-generalcy at Havana, an office altogether familiar with African slavery and with slave vendors' markets, which were so commonplace as to be characteristic of many Caribbean cultures. Though Spanish law did not, any more than French law had, recognize free days for slaves, in practice Spanish

[20]In addition to the *New Orleans Architecture* series cited in note 16 above, see Samuel Wilson, Jr., *Bienville's New Orleans: A French Colonial Capital, 1718-1768* (New Orleans, 1968). The *New Orleans City Guide* (New York, 1952), compiled by a number of first-rate historians in the 1930s under WPA auspices, can also prove useful. And historical maps and plans are indispensable. There are great numbers of them in various repositories: the manuscripts division of the libraries of the University of New Orleans, Tulane, LSU, the Louisiana State Museum Library in New Orleans (the old Cabildo collection), the New Orleans Public Library, and The Historic New Orleans Collection. In using such maps one must be careful not to confuse engineers' idealized conceptual renderings, which are useless save as studies in the history of city-planning theory, with maps and plans of the city as it actually existed at any given point. And even the best maps also sometimes have errors.

governing authorities, like the French authorities before them, respected such days as a matter of common-sense necessity.

Similarly, the market, which simply represented the embodiment of some of the slaves' free-day activities, enjoyed only informal recognition. It is true that during the Spanish period a number of free colored vendors almost certainly came to participate in the market alongside the bondsmen and that the authorities could have subjected such free vendors to commercial regulations. But, by and large, the market remained a slave activity, and, as such, had no standing in law. Spanish administrators, as much given to leaving bureaucratic paper trails to justify, and cover, their actions as their French predecessors, obviously could not officially regulate something that did not officially exist. Thus, while New Orleans's Spanish colonial records were filled with numerous, detailed regulations on the other markets and vendors of the city, none applied to the slave vendors.

Indeed, the most basic and comprehensive of such regulations, the 1784 ordinance on markets and marketing, expressly exempted from its provisions—in language carefully constructed so as to avoid a legal paradox—all "slaves belonging to private citizens who have their farms in the City" and "those sent daily from the country by their masters to sell their vegetables, milk, wild fowl, quartered venison, and mutton." Such slaves, the ordinance went on to say, "will continue to enjoy the liberty to sell their commodities in the City as they did before."[21]

The slave vendors also suffered little from competition with the complex of centralized market facilities the Spanish constructed in three stages between 1779 and 1784—and rebuilt a number of times afterwards, finally to achieve the form we know today as the French Market. The new central market spread along the Mississippi on the opposite side of town, and its wholesalers and retailers dealt mainly in much more standard

[21]Ordinances of September 10, 1784, "Records and Deliberations of the Cabildo, 1769-1803," III, 19-21. John E. Harkins, "The Neglected Phase of Louisiana's Colonial History: The New Orleans Cabildo, 1769-1803" (Ph. D. dissertation, Memphis State University, 1967), pp. 197-254, has a good discussion of Spanish market regulations. See Usner, "Frontier Exchange," pp. 194-197.

commodities than the slave vendors did—beef, pork, fish, and bulk staples such as flour.[22]

There were, of course, during the Spanish regime, as there had been during the French years and would be in the American antebellum decades, periods of slave unrest and rebellion, almost always followed by periods of curtailment or repression of slave freedoms. While suppressions may have temporarily diminished the market, there is no indication that they seriously, much less permanently, blighted it.[23]

On the other hand, any number of crown pronouncements on slave control, if executed according to their letter, could have effectively ended the market. But as with many directives from the far-away homeland, local authorities enforced them selectively, if at all. The *Real Cedula* of 1789 presented, on paper, the greatest threat to the slave vendors. From the point of view of its authors, the new code guaranteed to slaves all the benefits and securities, earthly and heavenly, to be derived from having a place in a Spanish, Catholic, seigneurial regime. The very first of its fourteen articles forbade slaves ever again to work on Sundays. That was the Lord's day, and on it one could work only for Him, not for any man, not even oneself. The remaining articles of the code went on to prohibit slaves from growing their own food, purchasing their own clothes, visiting off their plantations for assemblies or dances, mixing with members of the opposite sex on Sundays, working together in sexually mixed groups, or living together unless married by the church. All in all, it aimed at reducing slaves to a completely dependent caste.[24]

[22]Harkins, "The New Orleans Cabildo," pp. 206-217.

[23]Lynn C. Rouprich, "Slavery in Colonial Louisiana: The Politics of Repression" (M.A. thesis, University of New Orleans, 1983), while it lacks clear focus and full development, contains the germ of a provocative idea of cycles of slave revolts following periods of leniency and repression.

[24]The instructions sent to Louisiana by Charles III in 1776, while they contained a prohibition on slaves from different plantations congregating for meetings and dances, focused on preventing slave escapes, moderating punishments by masters, and on concubinage. On the much quoted, but often misinterpreted *Real Cedula*, see McGowan's informative discussion, "Creation of a Slave Society," pp. 262-295. Written permissions for slaves to work for others on off-days or to sell goods were called for in Spanish law and in the various crown and local governors' slave regulations as they had been in French law and regulations, but were rarely given by masters.

But it was clearly unworkable in Louisiana. The sitting governor, Esteban Miró, immediately sent off to his superiors his, the local *cabildo*'s, and local planters' advisements on the impracticality of attempting to enforce such regulations, and for the sixteen months remaining in his term, delayed implementation. His successor, the Baron de Carondelet, fearful lest the Caribbean island slave revolts inspired by the French Revolution spread to Louisiana and convinced that any moves toward slave repression would only increase the danger, simply ignored the *Real Cedula*, and in July of 1792 issued a slave code of his own. It, for the first time, expressly recognized slaves' rights to Sundays as free days.[25]

Another part of Carondelet's preparedness program consisted of strengthening the defenses of New Orleans. In the course of that, he rebuilt and enlarged the Orleans Bastion, making it, in 1792, into Fort Ferdinand. The brick-and-frame edifice covered much of the ground where the market had been, but it displaced the vendors only slightly, for they continued their sales at the foot of the fort's gorge, on the esplanade that replaced portions of the old trapezoidial "military" blocks.[26]

During the three decades after the Spanish took over Louisiana, New Orleans had spread outward towards its walls. The 1791 census listed thirty-five people in twelve households living on Rampart Street, "*la calle frente al bossu*," or the street in front of the woods. Negroes headed four of the households, mulattoes two, French Creoles five, and a Spanish sergeant one. The area, connected by a gateway in the wall to the terminus of the recently completed Carondelet navigation canal that ran

[25]Carondelet's Code, July 11, 1792. Transcripts of documents in the Archives of the Indies relating to Louisiana, Louisiana State University Library, Baton

[26]In addition to the works cited in notes 16 and 20 above, see Jerome A. Greene, "The Defense of New Orleans, 1718-1900," Jean Lafitte National Park Study, 1982, pp. 39-46. Carondelet's reports on the fortification of the city can be found in the Dispatches of Spanish Governors of Louisiana, the Louisiana State Museum Library, Book 1-A, p. 163, no. 13, L152-A. The slave song "*Pitis sans Popa*" enumerates a number of products brought into the city and sold by black vendors. While it is impossible to date this song's composition precisely, the form of its Creole French places it in the late eighteenth or early nineteenth century. See George Washington Cable, *Creoles and Cajuns: Stories of Old Louisiana*, ed. by Arlin Turner (New York, 1959), pp. 410-411.

from the city to the Bayou St. John, contained a mixture of working-class residents and service-, food-, and transport-oriented businesses. Occupations of the residents included soldiers, "travelers," gravediggers, farmers, coopers, hunters, warehousemen, draymen, carpenters, and hospital workers.[27]

Following Carondelet's administration and the short terms of three succeeding governors, Spain returned the colony to France in 1803, and twenty-one days later France handed it over to the United States. The Louisiana Purchase inaugurated the second and most important phase of Congo Square's history. The flood of Americans into Louisiana and New Orleans raised unprecedented problems of adjustment. For the first time in its history the United States faced the challenge of integrating a sizable non-Anglo-Saxon cultural group into the twenty-seven-year-old republic. And, conversely, Louisiana's French Creole culture, concentrated in New Orleans, faced the problem of accommodating, or accommodating to, the Anglo-Americans and the Anglo-American republic. While the city, during its long colonial history, had accommodated a number of other incoming cultural groups—the Indians, the Africans, some Germans, and a few Spaniards—it had never had to deal with anything like the numbers, assertiveness, determination, or sheer foreignness represented by the American invasion.

The first American governor, William C. C. Claiborne, immediately ordered the removal of New Orleans's old fortifications in order to open the city to its adjoining countryside in the typical U. S. fashion. As soon as the local population heard rumors of the removal project, they themselves largely dismantled the decayed palisade wall for firewood during the winter of 1804. What remained, including the three forts on the back side of town, Claiborne had pulled down early in 1805, leaving only the two forts on the river, which stood until 1808 and 1821.[28]

[27]The 1791 census, in the New Orleans Public Library, is arranged by streets, and, from the known sites one can determine the route followed by the enumerator, a serpentine one up and down the cross-streets. The above tabulations are drawn from the residents living near the ends of Orleans and adjacent streets.

[28]Greene, "The Defense of New Orleans," pp. 58, 98, plus the report, probably written by Edward Livingston, "The Political Situation of New Orleans in 1808,"

The slave merchants continued their market on the enlarged open space created by the demolition of Fort St. Ferdinand. In 1812 the city authorities subdivided the old Commons and an adjoining large tract of land they had purchased two years earlier from Paul-Claude-Joseph Tremé. They extended the city's short streets across Rampart into the new area and cut a range of new long streets paralleling Rampart. In the process they reserved the spot where Fort St. Ferdinand had stood—the block bounded by Rampart, St. Claude, and St. Ann streets on three sides and by the Carondelet Canal turning basin on the fourth—for public use, as they did a number of other parcels of land in the new subdivision. Governor Claiborne had earlier explained to President Thomas Jefferson that preserving several open squares and laying out and improving several public walks would not only "beautify the town, but contribute greatly to the health and comfort of the inhabitants."[29]

A number of the reserved spaces and promenades, particularly the one along the outer reaches of the Carondelet Canal, planted with trees, sweet-smelling shrubs, and flowers, did, indeed, add to the comfort of the residents and the beauty of New Orleans. But the area of the city around the site of old Fort St. Ferdinand retained its commercial, transport, and service character. That site, lying next to the turning basin, always full of boats loaded with onions, turnips, collards, oysters, and shrimp, could never have been made into a leisure park. Instead the city fathers designated it *Place Publique* and left it a simple, open, grassy plain. But few would call the spot *Place Publique* for long. Circumstances gave rise to other, more popular, names.[30]

For a number of years after about 1816, a certain Signore Gaetano "from Havana," immortalized as "Monsieur Cayetano" in George Cable's most famous short story, "Posson

---

Louisiana Historical Quarterly, XI (1928), 378-379. Fort St. Louis was demolished in 1808 and Fort St. Charles in 1821.

[29]Dunbar Rowland, ed., *Official Letter Books of W. C. C. Claiborne*, 6 vols. (Jackson, Miss., 1921), letter of December 22, 1804; Toledano and Christovich, *Faubourg Tremé*, pp. 62-63.

[30]The *Place Publique* designation appears on the maps of the time.

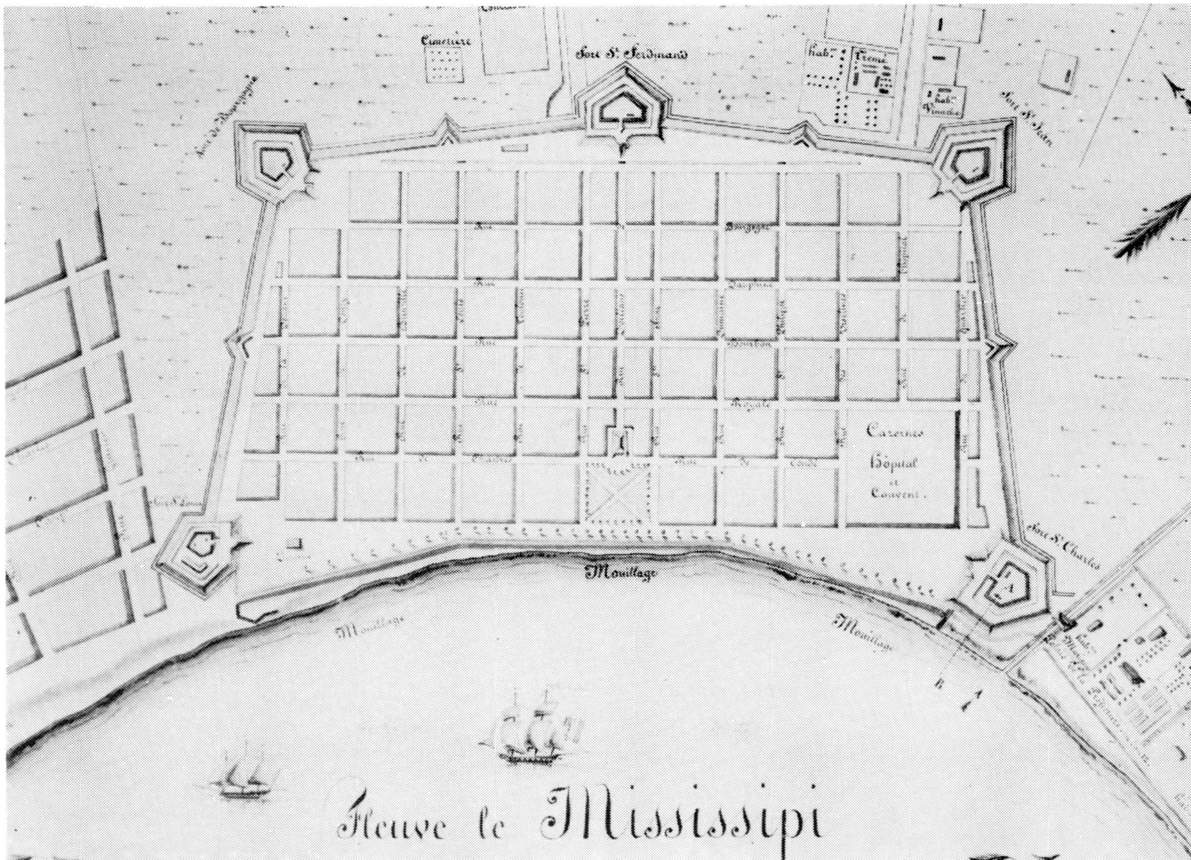

Figure 1 Detail from 1803 *Plan de la ville Orleans* by Joseph Vinache, showing Fort Saint Ferdinand, at the foot of which, inside the city walls, the Congo Square vendors displayed their wares and held their Sunday dances. (*Historic New Orleans Collection*)

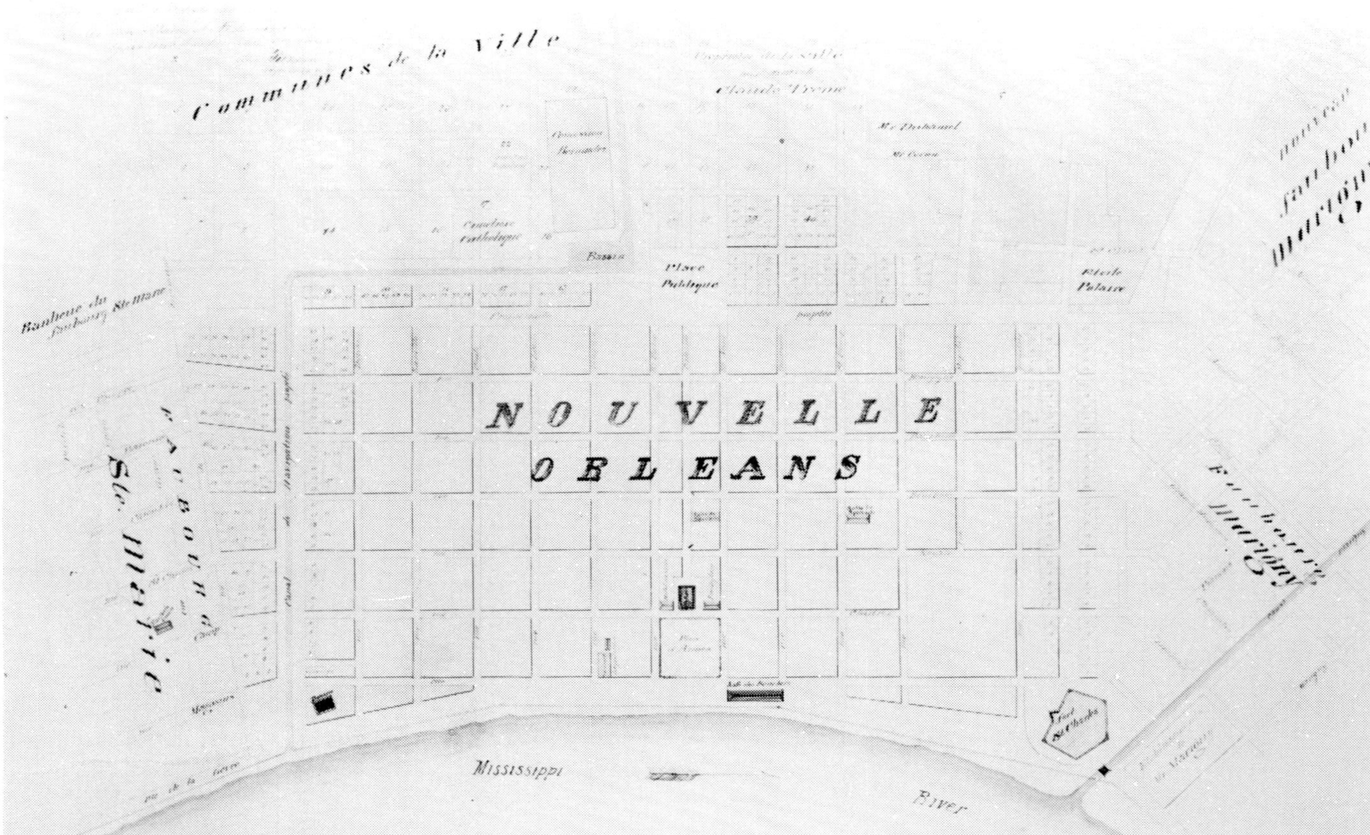

Figure 2 Detail from 1812 *Plan de la ville* by Jacques Tanesse, showing the city after the old walls and forts were removed and new suburbs platted where the old City Commons had been. Congo Square is here called *Place Publique*. (*Historic New Orleans Collection)*

Figure 3 A view of Congo Square today. The rings formed by the paving stones are reminiscent of the dance circles Benjamin Latrobe saw on the same spot nearly two hundred hears ago.

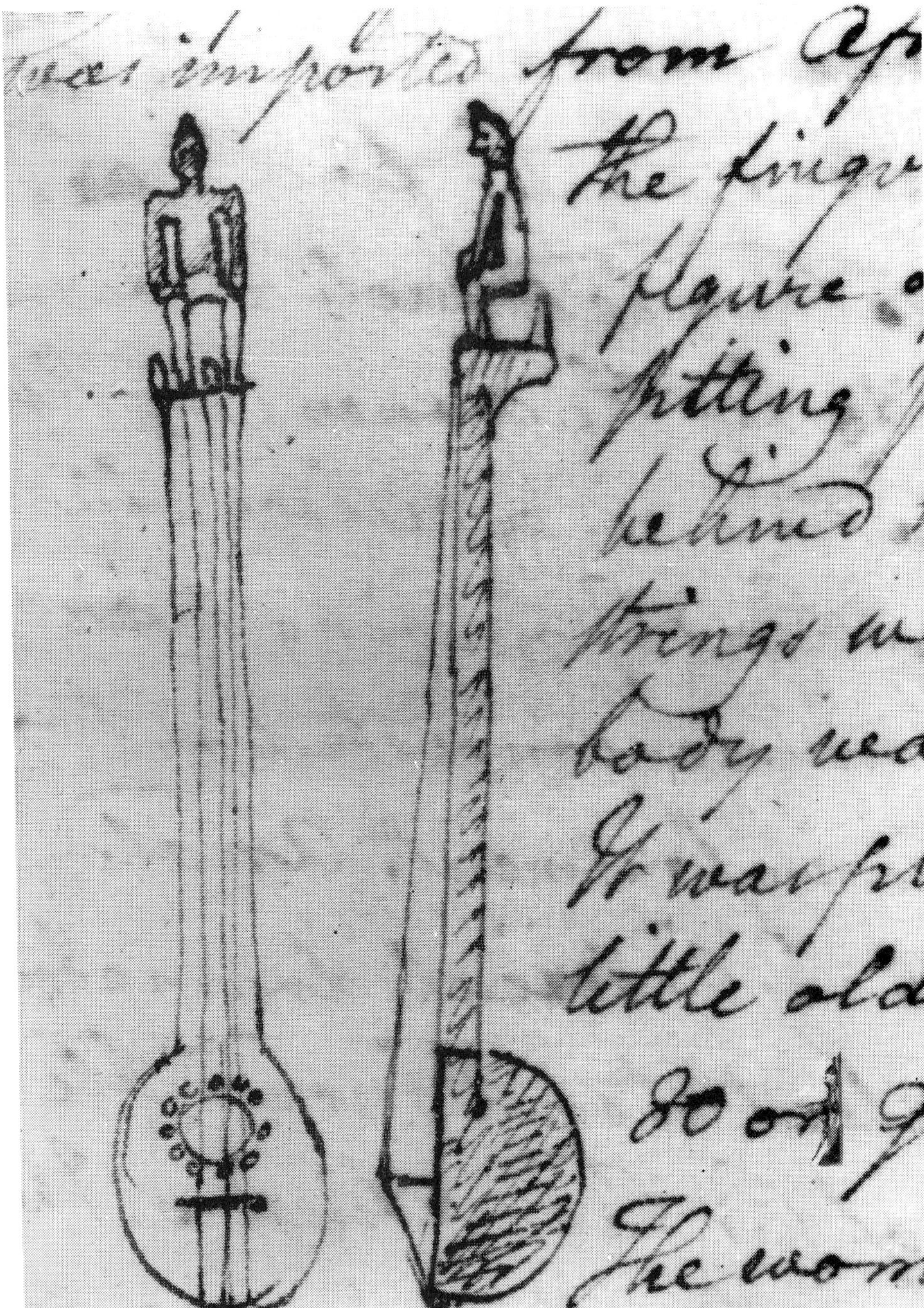

Figure 4 Drawings by the distinguished architect/engineer, Benjamin Henry Latrobe, of a stringed instrument which he saw being played for dances on Congo Square when he was in New Orleans in 1819. It is a *banjer*, or long-necked lute, of African origin: (*Maryland Historical Society, Baltimore*)

Figure 5 B.H. Latrobe's drawings of several musical instrument used to accompany dancers in Congo Square in 1819. These are an *ogororo*, or slit-drum, a stool-shaped square drum, and a nail-studded calabash, all of African origin. (*Maryland Historical Society, Baltimore*)

Figure 6 B.H. Latrobe's drawings of two drums used to accompany dancers in Congo Square in 1819. They are a *congaa* and an open-staved drum; both are of African origin. (*Maryland Historical Society, Baltimore*)

Figure 7 An artist's conception of the old dances in Congo Square, made by E.W. Kemble in 1885 and based on George Washington Cable's description of the earlier dances.

Figure 8 Two more of E.W. Kemble's 1885 conceptual drawings of what an earlier Congo Square dance, "The Love Song," and a "Fiddler" may have looked like.

Figure 9 E.W. Kemble's **1885** portrait drawings of two black New Orleanians, one representing "Calalou," a young quadroon featured in a creole love song popular in early New Orleans and the other representing the typical physiognomy of a Mandingo man. Note the tuft of hair secured at the nape of the neck by a leather thong.

Figure 10 E.W. Kemble's 1885 drawing of a "Candjo," a creole word used in early songs to distinguish Louisiana-born men of pure African ancestry from those of mixed, African and European or African and Indian ancestry. Note the tribal facial tattoos.

Notes on the Drawings of Benjamin Henry Latrobe

By John Joyce

Benjamin Henry Latrobe (1764-1820) was a well educated architect/engineer when he came to the United States from England in 1796. Often considered the first professional architect in the United States, his commissions included important buildings in Philadelphia, Baltimore and Washington, D.C., where he supervised and redesigned aspects of the U.S. Capitol and the White House. An acute observer, his journals, drawings and watercolors record his impressions. He came to New Orleans in 1819 to supervise the development of a city waterworks, and died there of yellow fever on September 3, 1820.

Latrobe's reference to Negro musical instruments is of more than passing interest. Before the present century and the advent of ethnomusicology, our knowledge of the music of sub-Saharan Africa was virtually nil. As a consequence, written descriptions of African instruments in the New World, scarce enough before Latrobe's account in 1819, are usually of a bewildered and inexplicit nature. By contrast, Latrobe, with his artist's eye for detail, gives us precise descriptions of both the instruments and the manner in which they are played, accompanied by accurate drawings. These provide a small but concrete piece of evidence concerning the demographic status of the slave population in antebellum Louisiana. By comparing Latrobe's drawings with the systematic mappings of African instruments compiled by such ethnomusicologists as Eric von Hornbostle and Curt Sachs, we can define with a fair degree of accuracy the particular region of West Africa from which these instruments derive and, thus, which tribal groups brought them to Louisiana.

The six instruments described by Latrobe include three membranophones (drum types), two idiophones (non-drum percussion types), and a chordophone (stringed type). While variants of all these instruments can be found throughout much of West Africa, the specific instrument designs pictured by Latrobe can be tied to more particular areas. For example, the cylindrical drum played with the hands in "hobby horse" position is a specific form of hand drum called the conga, local to the coastal nation of Nigeria, where it is the chief drum of the Yoruban tribe. Also Yoruban is the "cricket bat" instrument, a hand held form of slit drum (or slit gong) called an ogororo; it was in common use among descendants of Yorubans in Cuba in the nineteenth and twentieth centuries. The stool-shaped square drum, on the other hand, is a type used by the Ijaw tribe of southeast Nigeria and also by the chief tribe of Ghana, the Ashanti; it is still used by Ashanti descendants in Jamaica. The open-staved drum resembling a small table is identical to one found among the Aradas of Dahomey. The nail-studded calabash is basic over a wide range of West Africa, including Angola, Zaire, Cameroon, Nigeria, and Ghana. The "curious" stringed instrument is a long-neck African lute with a taut animal skin across the open top of the calabash shell body. This instrument, found in variant forms in Zaire, Cameroon, Nigeria, Dahomey, and Ghana, is the West-African prototype of the modem American banjo. Given its broad African range, it is not surprising that it was to be found among slaves in the Anglo-American colonies of the Atlantic seaboard as well as in Louisiana and the West Indies. In Anglo colonies the instrument was called banjer, banjar, or strum-strum. It is mentioned by Thomas Jefferson in his *Notes on Virginia* (Paris, 1784) as "the most common stringed instrument among the slaves."

The provenance of these various instruments ties perfectly into the early history of New Orleans, which was, successively, a French, Spanish, and Anglo-American city.

The bulk of the slaves brought there by the French were from Dahomey. The great majority of Spanish-owned slaves were Yorubans from Nigeria, by way of Cuba and, after 1803, the Anglo-Americans brought, from the Southern plantations, Ashantis from Ghana. It would appear that. at a musical level, interaction of these separate tribal cultures had begun.

By 1886, when George Washington Cable wrote about Congo Square ("Dance in Place Congo," *Century Magazine*, February 1886), a further stage of interaction was taking place. Cable saw hollowed log drums sat upon and "beaten on the skin madly with the fingers, fists, and feet;" a pebble-filled gourd shell "flourished violently at the end of a stout staff with one hand and beaten upon the palm of the other," Other performers scraped "the jawbone of some ox, horse, or mule...with a long key;" and still others beat "empty barrels...with the shankbones of cattle." Thus far, this description could apply equally to West Africa or the West Indies. But Cable mentions several new, non-African instruments: performers who "rang triangles" and others who "twanged jew's harps" and "blew Pan's pipes." Finally, Cable observed a commercial banjo "with four strings." It is clear that, some twenty years after the end of slavery, acculturation had taken place between Afro-Americans and Euro-Americans. It was in this same decade (1880s) that the first black brass bands were formed in New Orleans, a critical step in the genesis of jazz.

Note on the Illustrations of E. W. Kemble

Edward Windsor Kemble (1861-1933) was a noted illustrator whose work often appeared, from 1881 on, in magazines such as the old Life, Colliers, Century, Harper's Weekly, and Leslie's. He also published a dozen or so books of his drawings. He specialized in depicting African-Americans, but unlike most of his contemporaries, his drawings were often carefully done portraits, rather than caricatures. Hence his work sometimes takes on a particular historical significance.

Born in Sacramento, California, Kemble came to New Orleans in 1885, attracted as many journalists and illustrators were, to the World's Industrial and Cotton Centennial Exposition that had opened in the city a few months earlier. Over the next twelve years, until 1897, Kemble visited the city often, each time making more drawings.

All of his works reproduced here were done during his initial visit to New Orleans in 1885, and all were to illustrate two of George Washington Cable's articles in Century Magazine, "The Dance in Congo Square" (February 1886) and "Creole Slave Songs" (April 1886). The cover illustration of the present volume, "Congo Woman," is clearly a portrait, as are his "Calalou," his "Mandingo," and his "Candjo," also reproduced here. Likely, local subjects were recommended to Kemble as representative of these types of black New Orleanians. "The Bamboula" and "Love Song" dance scenes and "The Fiddler," on the other hand, are more hypothetical. Though in its essentials probably not misleading, the Bamboula dance scene, for example, is little more than an artist's conception based on the description of the old dances given in Cable's article which the drawing was designed to illustrate. Indeed, the spires of St. Louis Cathedral in the background of the scene are anachronistic, for they were added to the structure only in 1851, a good twenty years after the heyday of the wild Congo Square dances that Kemble depicts.

Jone'," seasonally set up in the square his celebrated, and controversial, Congo Circus. Lafcadio Hearn said the circus became a "popular fixture" of New Orleans life, still remembered, or thought to be remembered, by New Orleanians when he was writing about it sixty years later.

To the perturbation of black New Orleanians, the Congo Circus admitted only whites. In order to facilitate collecting entrance fees as well as keeping Negroes out, the city authorities, in 1820, fenced in the square with wooden railings, leaving only two turnstile gates. Restricted to following the circus's entrance parade to its site, helping with the setting up, and then to hanging on the fence rails in hopes of a glimpse at the exotica in the square, the disappointed black Creoles made up a singular ditty about the circus. Its nineteen lines built up through a description of the circus's delights to end with the more than faintly bitter irony that "they would not show to black folks" what they showed to "*dotchians* and *dos-brilés*," the Creole *patois* words for white trash and rednecks, literally, "dogbacks" and "burnt-backs."

In addition to a man who danced in a sack, one who danced on his hands, one who stood on the back of a galloping horse while drinking a glass of champagne, a "pretty young lady" bareback rider, and a monkey handler, the Congo Circus sported a tiny, four-horse carrousel and featured fights between Signore Gaetano's champion bear and tiger and local bulls and dogs. The fights, as one of Gaetano's newspaper advertisements promised, furnished "a very entertaining amusement." But the fights also provided an occasion for laying wagers, and marked the beginning of the square's long association with illicit gambling.[31]

[31]The city fathers also "beautified" the square in 1820 with some scraggly young sycamores and elms. On the square at this period and on the Congo Circus see George Adams Paxton, *The New Orleans Directory and Register* (New Orleans, 1823), p. 139; Henry C. Castellanos, *New Orleans As It Was: Episodes of Louisiana Life,* ed by George F. Reinecke (Baton Rouge, 1978), pp. 19, 157; Lafcadio Hearn's section in the *Historical Sketch Book and Guide to New Orleans and Environs* (New Orleans, 1885), pp. 297-298; Mary Cable, *Lost New Orleans* (Boston, 1980), pp. 183-184; George W. Cable, "Creole Slave Songs," *Century Magazine,* XXXI (1886), 807-828; and the useful article on "The Congo Dance," *Kunkel's Musical Review,* II (1884), which was reprinted from an original article that appeared in the New Orleans *Daily Picayune*, October 12, 1879. The *patois* word Hearn transcribed as *dochans*, Cable transcribed as *dotchians.* Circuses and circus performers, even more than prizefights and

In a quite different way the *Place Publique*'s long remembered association with the Congo Circus and its still longer, and continuing, association with New Orleans's old black community coalesced with its striking physical appearance—a starkly bare open field in the middle of an otherwise lushly overgrown city—to give rise to its famous name. While official documents continued to refer to it as *Place Publique*, the city's population, after the Congo Circus began repeatedly setting up there in 1816, increasingly called the spot *Place du Cirque*, Circus Park, and Circus Square. So common did those appellations become, at least among the white sector, that by the 1830s official documents routinely used them. On the other hand, slaves and free people of color, who generally called the Congo Circus simply "the Congo," also began to call the fairground "Congo Plain(s)" and "Congo Square." Those names gained in popularity, especially as the square's African dances, including one called the Congo, became occasions for outings by local residents as well as tourists. and bv 1850 occasionally also began to appear in official records, alongside *Place du Cirque* and "Circus Square." Then in the 1870s and 1880s, two things tipped the balance in favor of "Congo Plain(s)" and "Congo Square." George Washington Cable, fascinated with the African component of the square's history, used those names in his widely read articles, stories, and novels. And about the same time, a multitude of guidebook and newspaper writers, in New Orleans for the Cotton Exposition of 1884-1885, picked up the terms. Their writings, occurring amid the surge of self-awareness generated in New Orleans by the national attention focused on the city by the Exposition, fixed those names in the New Orleans vocabulary for all time. The Exposition awakened New Orleanians to the reality that their town was, in so very many ways, different from any other American city, and that the difference was something to be proud of.[32]

---

prizefigthers, which appeal mostly to men, take an extraordinarily lasting hold on the popular mind, a phenomenon that has not yet been adequately explained. There are many people today, for example, who will say, believingly, that they remember seeing Tom Thumb, while the fact of the matter is that no one alive can remember the Little General who retired from public appearances in 1882 and died a year later.

[32]See below notes 47-50. The works of Cable and the various guidebook writers are cited numerous times above and below. Paxton was already singling out the

The Faubourg Tremé, as the area stretching back from Congo Square came to be called, was from the beginning racially mixed, with blacks and whites living side by side. The faubourg constituted antebellum New Orleans's largest and most important free-colored neighborhood. The number of free people of color in the city had jumped from an insignificant ninety-nine at the end of the French period to over thirteen hundred at the time of the Louisiana Purchase. And by the Civil War it had grown to nearly 19,000, far and away the largest concentration in the Deep South. The city's free people of color, while they had skins of all hues and shades, remained overwhelmingly French-speaking, Catholic Creoles. Most made their livings as day laborers, dock and construction workers, washerwomen, and servants; some as skilled masons, plasterers, carpenters, and metal workers: some as street vendors, caterers, nurses, midwives, seamstresses, hairdressers, barbers, and musicians; and a few as businessmen, money lenders, and planters. In the Faubourg Tremé most of the free-colored population not only lived but also established the city's major free-black schools, benevolent associations, social clubs, and literary and musical societies. Consequently, Congo Square's Sunday crowds came virtually entirely from the city's Creole community. Few came from the English-speaking black community, which lived well uptown from the square.[33]

If Congo Square attracted the lower orders from all over New Orleans to its coarse carnival, circus, and bearbaiting spectacles, it also served as the Faubourg Tremé's public meeting ground. During the circus and carnival off-season,

---

Congo dancers for special attention as early as 1823, though he called the site the "Circus Public Square," combining two of its usual names. See his *Directory*, p. 139. The *Place d'Armes*, now Jackson Square, also remained "a parched sterile" military assembly ground until it was landscaped in the 1850s, but generally the city was lush with vegetation.

[33]Toledano and Christovich's *Faubourg Tremé*, pp. 85-107, is a particularly good treatment of the social aspects of the neighborhood. "Faubourg" for suburb is one of the many Gallicisms remaining in New Orleans speech today, though it, like many, is pronounced in an English fashion. Castellanos, *New Orleans As It Was*, p. 158, noted that most of the square's crowd was Creole, overstating his point by adding that the "*nègres 'Mericains* were not invited," for there was "no affinity" between the Creole and American black groups.

neighborhood youths used the square as a playing field, particularly for *raquettes*, a lacrosse-like Choctaw Indian game that remained popular in New Orleans throughout the nineteenth century. The slave and free-black vendors continued to set up there on Sunday morning, and to mingle with the crowds of other slaves and free blacks who gathered on Sunday afternoons for the square's famous, and historically significant, African dances.

The Americans who flooded into New Orleans during the decades following the Purchase found themselves fascinated and not infrequently appalled by what they saw. The large number of free people of color, some bearing arms and most consorting intimately with slaves, who themselves appeared to enjoy a degree of freedom of movement and action unprecedented in the rest of the South, made many of the incoming Americans, including Governor Claiborne, extremely nervous. They had never seen anything like it. Nor had most seen anything like the way French, Catholic New Orleans observed the Sabbath. After going to mass on Sunday morning, the Creoles made the rest of the day a festival, indulging themselves in public entertainments, going on outings and excursions, enjoying picnics and barbecues, shopping the street markets, and, on Sunday evenings, drinking and dancing. It struck the newcomers, mostly Anglo-Protestants accustomed to taking Sundays as days of grim abstinence and pious reflection, as near blasphemy.

The Sunday dances in Congo Square, which represented the most important aspect of its history, at the time also served, more than any other single facet of New Orleans life, to focus the Anglo-American concern and indignation. Benjamin Latrobe's reaction was typical. What he saw in the square prompted him to write a long and altogether disapproving entry in his journal—a "dissertation," he called it—on the Creole mode of Sunday observance. And he betrayed his amazement and apprehension at the sight of five or six hundred unsupervised slaves assembled for dancing when he added, in a tone of relief, "there was not the least disorder among the crowd, nor do I learn on enquiry, that these weekly meeting of negroes have ever produced any mischief."[34] But at the same time, he,

[34]Latrobe, *Impressions Respecting New Orleans*, pp. 46-49.

and observers like him, found themselves drawn into fascination with the dancing they saw, for they had never seen anything like it either.

What they saw was not merely groups of slaves and free people of color dancing. Such was a common enough sight throughout the South. They saw something in New Orleans that had not been seen elsewhere in North America for nearly a century, native African music and dance still being performed. And that was what so fascinated the observers. Such African music and dance elsewhere had long before acculturated to Anglo-American norms, or, under pressure from Protestant preachers, black as well as white, had eroded. "Only in Place Congo in New Orleans was the African tradition able to continue in the open," concluded Dena J. Epstein from her masterful examination of antebellum black folk music.[35]

African dances had been performed on the Congo Plains, as well as at other locations in the city, and on some plantations, since the importation of slaves began in the 1720s. But because of the Congo Plain's long association with a market function out of which the dancing grew—the way vendors and their friends wiled away the day between their occasional sales—that location became, and remained, a particular focal point for such dancing. Indeed the law itself helped make it such. Five years after the Purchase, the 1808 New Orleans Police Code, repeated in an 1817 ordinance, forbade such dancing "except on Sundays, at such places only as may be therefore appointed by the Mayor, and no where else."[36]

[35]*Sinful Tunes and Spirituals: Black Folk Music to the Civil War* (Chicago, 1977), pp. 84-85. This work, plus her two articles, "Slave Music in the United States Before 1860: A Survey of Sources," *Notes*, XX (1963), 195-212, 377-390; and "African Music in British and French America," *The Musical Quarterly*, LIX (1973), 61-91; along with Kmen's *Music in New Orleans: The Formative Years, 1781-1841* cite virtually all known references to the African dancing in Congo Square, most of which also note the New Orleans observance of Sundays and, often, the apprehension at large crowds of unsupervised slaves. See also Ira Berlin's important article, "Time, Space, and the Evolution of Afro-American Society on British Mainland North America," *American Historical Review*, LXXXV (1980), 44-78. Gary A. Donaldson, "A Window on Slave Culture: Dances at Congo Square in New Orleans, 1800-1862," *Journal of Negro History*, LXIX (1984), adds nothing new, nor does David C. Estes, "Traditional Dances and Processions of Blacks in New Orleans as Witnessed by Antebellum Travelers," *Louisiana Folklore Miscellany*, VI (1990), 1-14.

[36]Even after the French period, during which virtually all of Louisiana's slaves had come directly from Africa, great numbers continued to come directly,

That colonial observers and visitors to the colony took no notice of the African dancing should not be surprising. Governor Miró's 1786 ban on such dancing during church hours was one of the rare mentions.[37] Most French and Spanish visitors to colonial New Orleans came by way of the Caribbean islands and would have viewed such dances, as they viewed the slaves' market itself, as too commonplace to deserve note. And the relatively few English and American visitors were mostly businessmen, or spies, interested in commercial operations and military defenses, not in cultural curiosities.[38] But with the incoming Anglo-Americans after the Purchase it was entirely different. Hence the sudden flood of comments during the early decades of the nineteenth century.

In addition to the various drums, gourds, sounding boxes, and banjo-like instruments that Latrobe saw, other observers noted the Congo Square musicians blowing cow-horn hunting crooks and "quillpipes" made from reeds strung together like panpipes, playing marimbas, scraping the teeth of horses' jawbones with sticks, and having adopted European instruments such as violins, tambourines, triangles, and cremonas.[39] They described the dancers as "dressed in a

---

without any "seasoning" in the Caribbean islands. For the police regulations of March 14, 1808, see *Police Code, or Collection of the Ordinances of Police Made by the City Council of New Orleans* (New Orleans, 1808), pp. 48-50. Kmen, *Music in New Orleans*, p. 227, noted the October 15, 1817 ordinance.

[37]Governor Miró's 1786 *Bando de Buen Gobierno* cited by Roger Baudier, *The Catholic Church in Louisiana* (New Orleans, 1939), p. 203. Epstein, *Sinful Tunes*, pp. 91-92, cites the few other mentions of dancing in the colonial period.

[38]Joseph G. Tregle, Jr., "British Spy Along the Mississippi: Thomas Hutchins and the Defense of New Orleans, 1773," *Louisiana History*, VIII (1967), 313-327, furnishes a typical example.

[39]Castellanos, *New Orleans As It Was*, p. 297, understandably mistook the hunting crooks for "wooden horns shaped like those of a cow" because such horn crooks, aged and oiled from constant handling, do indeed take on a texture and graining closely resembling that of wood. He, along with a number of others, including Cable and Hearn, mentioned the jawbones. Cable in his "Dance in Place Congo," 519-521, mentioned the simple marimba and the quill pipes. James R. Creecy noted the violins and triangles in his *Scenes in the South, and Other Miscellaneous Pieces* (Washington, D. C., 1860), pp. 19-23. The New Orleans *Daily Picayune*, October 18, 1843, mentioned *la petite tambour*; and on March 22, 1846, the "Cremona," probably a Jew's harp. The *Daily Picayune* of March 22, 1846, mentioned that onlookers threw coins to the musicians.

variety of wild and savage fashions . . . ornamented with a number of tails of the smaller wild beasts," with "fringes, ribbons, little bells, and shells and balls, jingling and flirting about the performers' legs and arms." The women, one onlooker reported, wore, "each according to her means," the "newest fashions in silk, gauze, muslin, percale dresses." And the males clothed themselves in "oriental and Indian dress" with "Turkish" turbans of red, blue, yellow, green and brown and covered themselves only with a "sash of the same sort wrapped around the body . . . except for that they go naked."[40]

One witness also made the observation that the several clusters of onlookers, musicians, and dancers in Congo Square represented, in the early decades, tribal groupings, "each nation taking their place in different parts of the square." "The Minahs," he continued, "would not dance near the Congos, nor the Mandringos near the Gangas," and often fights broke out between the groups. Some of the males, he said, still bore facial tattoos and had filed teeth.[41]

The dances themselves, at least some of them, mounted from a slow, repetitious, and grimly deliberate opening phase—the only phase Latrobe stayed in Congo Square long enough to see—in an increasingly lascivious crescendo to a final frenzy of "fantastic leaps" in which "ecstasy rises to madness," and

[40]Christian Schultz, Jr., *Travels on an Inland Voyage Through the States of New-York, Pennsylvania, Virginia, Ohio, Kentucky, and Tennessee, and Through the Territories of Indiana, Louisiana, Mississippi and New Orleans: Performed in the Years 1807 and 1808 . . .*, 2 vols. (New York, 1810), II, 197; Creecy, *Scenes in the South*; Johann Beuchler, *Land und Seereisen eines St. Gallischen Kantonsburgers nach Nordamerika und Westindien uber Amsterdam nach Baltimore, Pitzburg, Gallipoli Sensanetta, Neu-Vevay, die Gegend Wabasch am Ohio, Natschet, Battonrouge und New-Orleans . . . 1816, 1817 und 1818 . . .* (St. Gallen, 1820), pp.129-130, quoted in Epstein, *Sinful Tunes*, p. 95. The October 12, 1879, *Daily Picayune* article later reprinted in *Kunkel's Musical Review* notes that many of the slaves seen in Congo Square had been smuggled into Louisiana from Africa well after such imports became illegal in 1808. The small metal discs some observers noted many of the dancers and members of the crowd wearing around their necks or ankles were, in most cases, simply small silver coins that had been holed and strung on thongs, a common slave practice throughout the South. The University of New Orleans has a collection of such slave jewelry.

[41]The same 1879 *Daily Picayune* writer cited above. See Loren Schweninger, ed., *Tennessee Slave to St. Louis Entrepreneur: The Autobiography of James Thomas* (Columbia, Mo., 1984), pp. 49, 109.

finally, suddenly, the dancers fell, exhausted and unconscious, "foam on their lips," and were "dragged out of the circle by their arms and legs" as new dancers took their place, the music never ceasing.[42]

Such dances, or at least similar dances, had earlier been associated with voodoo on the Congo Plain. But as the city grew out to encompass Congo Square, voodooists moved their rites to more isolated locations, first to abandoned houses on the old Bayou Road and to cabins along the outer limits of the newly opened but still largely uninhabited Elysian Fields Avenue, later to a spot they called "The Camp" on the edge of Bayou St. John, and finally to the swampy environs of Lake Pontchartrain. It was at the latter location that famed "voodoo queen" Marie Laveau held forth in the 1870s, and there that Lafcadio Hearn witnessed a voodoo ceremony in the early 1880s.[43]

[42]This description is drawn largely from Cable's "Dance in Place Congo" and Hearn's "Scenes of Cable's Romances," *Century Magazine*, XXXVII (November 1883), 45, and must be taken as generalized. Both Cable and Hearn were capable and careful historical researchers; see Turner's comments in his *George W. Cable*, pp. 228-235, and *passim*, and above, note 15. For his description of the Congo Square dances Cable relied heavily on Médéric Louis Elie Moreau de Saint-Méry's *Description topographique, physyque, civile, politique et historique de la partie française de l'Isle Saint-Domingue*, 2 vols. (Philadelphia, 1797-1798), and the same author's *De la danse* (Parma, 1801), both of which were second-hand descriptions of Saint-Domingue dances. However carefully Cable used these works, probably to fill in details lacking in the descriptions of Congo Square dances he gleaned from elderly New Orleanians, the fact remains that he was writing long after the dances ceased in Congo Square and using some materials from a questionable source. Thus while Cable's descriptions probably are not misleading in their essentials, they have to be used with care.

[43]Thanks to the work of Joseph Logsdon of the University of New Orleans, we can now distinguish between the two women named Marie Laveau, mother and daugther, who have been confused one for the other since Cable mistook the mother for the daugther in his "Creole Slave Songs," *Century Magazine*, XXXI (April 1886), 807-828. The elder Marie, known for her good works, visiting, feeding, and nursing inmates of the parish prison, broke with her daugther, the "voodoo queen," to be reconciled only when she was nearly a hundred years old and too infirm to any longer care for herself. She died in 1881. The younger Marie, a hairdresser by profession; died in 1890 at the age of seventy-five and was buried in St. Louis II Cemetery, not in the St. Louis I tomb that voodoo fanciers regularly today mark with signs and decorate with offerings, or even in the top vault of row 25, St. James Aisle of St. Louis II, which also sometimes receives offerings, but in the second vault from the top of nearby row 19, on the same aisle. See the brochure, *Black History Tour of St. Louis Cemetery, Square 3* (New

On the other hand, the traditional Sunday activities in Congo Square continued, though not unaltered. The opening of a centralized vegetable vending facility in the French Market complex in 1823 began seriously to diminish the age-old marketing activities of Congo Square. Increased vending from market boats moored in the turning basin of the Carondelet Canal, which was deepened, widened, and extended all the way to the lake between 1832 and 1835, also cut into the slave vendors' business. And competition from the huge Tremé Market, which city authorities opened in 1839-40 two blocks away, effectively ended the square's history as a marketplace. Thenceforth only a few street vendors remained in Congo Square to peddle gingerbread, rice cakes, and pralines to the Sunday afternoon crowds. At the same time, the 1834 construction of the massive Parish Prison one block away blighted the square and its immediate neighborhood with a griminess that would last long after the prison itself disappeared.

The simple passage of time also wrought some important changes. By the 1830s and 1840s, the portion of the slave population born in Africa, and old enough to have learned the traditional dances of their motherlands, had shrunk significantly. And though they and younger generations continued the dances, more and more their steps and movements incorporated elements of European dance, a process that had begun much earlier, but which accelerated during the antebellum American decades of New Orleans's history. During the Mardi Gras celebration of 1808, for example, Pierre de Laussat, who had come to Louisiana to transfer the colony to the United States and had stayed on a few years, noted two circles of black dancers side by side, one group performing an African *bamboula* and the other a French *contre-danse*. In 1843 a local writer noted that many New Orleanians of the time had never seen the pure African dances. He had himself never seen them in the square, he said, but only once in the backyard of a private house, where two women and one man danced while four

---

Orleans, 1980), and the article based on Logsdon's research in the New Orleans *States-Item*, February 12, 1980, front page. On voodoo dancing, see Epstein, *Sinful Tunes*, p. 135. Much of the caution urged in the preceding note relative to the reliability of descriptions of the dances in Congo Square could be repeated relative to descriptions of New Orleans voodoo practices and ceremonies.

musicians played and chanted a "vocal chorus." Two years later Benjamin M. Norman also commented that the "unsophisticated" old "Congo" dances of the square's "primitive days" had ceased. And in 1879 a writer for the *Daily Picayune,* describing New Orleans as it was during his young manhood, noted the new, acculturated Afro-American dance forms emerging in the 1820s, 1830s, and 1840s, what he called the "imitations" got up by "the descendants of the original Africans." He insisted that the African dances, as distinct from the "imitations," continued in the square "until about 1819, but not later." All of which suggests that the 1820s saw the balance between traditional African dances and developing Afro-American dances tip in favor of the new forms.[44]

A number of factors allowed for the astonishingly long survival of traditional African dances in New Orleans: the high degree of tolerance and accommodation the French in the New World accorded sub-cultures generally; the city's isolation during its French colonial history; its Caribbean nexus formed during the thirty-four years Spain governed the colony; its geographical remoteness from the centers of United States culture for quite some time after the American purchase; the city's extraordinarily large African population, which outnumbered its European population from 1760 until 1840; and, not the least, the inordinate preoccupation of the city's French Creole host culture with dancing of all kinds, something remarked upon by observers more often even than they remarked upon the African dances themselves.[45]

[44]Pierre Clément de Laussat, *Mémoire sur ma vie, à mon fils, pendant les années 1803 et suivantes . . . à la Louisiane . . .* (Pau, 1831), p. 395. This is the same Laussat mentioned in note 15 above. *Daily Picayune*, October 18, 1843; Benjamin Moore Norman, *Norman's New Orleans and Environs* (New Orleans, 1845), p. 182. The October 12, 1879, *Daily Picayune* writer has been cited a number of times in the notes above.

[45]The last French census of the colonial period, done in 1763, showed the African population of the city and its environs, slave and free, having just come to outnumber the European colonists—4,621 to 4,566. See Jacqueline K. Voorhies, comp., *Some Late Eigtheenth-Century Louisianians: Census Records, 1758-1796* (Lafayette, La., 1973). In the state of Louisiana as a whole, blacks outnumbered whites until the Twelfth Census of the United States, 1900, showed whites outnumbering blacks, 729,612 to 650,804. The first chapter of Kmen's *Music in New Orleans* documents the Creole fetish for dancing, though it offers little explanation for it.

But, alone, the unusually long survival of African dances in New Orleans would be of no particular significance. They would represent only an historical curiosity. The real significance of the survival lies in the fact that it lasted long enough for an assimilation process, one peculiar to New Orleans, to take place. Indeed, survival is the wrong word, for it implies an eventual demise. And as Ira Berlin and others have pointed out, African culture in the New World did not die, nor was it lost or destroyed. It was transformed. Like the various European cultures transplanted to these shores, the many African cultures joined and blended with each other and with the European and the native American Indian cultures to become a new meld, Afro-American culture.[46]

The Afro-American meld that came out of Congo Square differed primarily, and importantly, in that it occurred not in the rural Anglo-Saxon Protestant setting that usually hosted the transformation process, but in a French, Creole, Catholic city recently become a part of the United States. That fact added what amounted to an extra, and subtly complex, step in the process. In New Orleans the formative stage of Afro-American culture involved a blending of African, Indian, and French, plus a few German and Spanish cultural elements. That peculiarly New Orleans black compound then blended with the greater Afro-American and American cultural meld being formed in the nation at large.

In the case in point, the dance forms that emerged in Congo Square were as uniquely a New Orleans product as was jazz. And those dances almost certainly made their way into the greater American culture via the same route New Orleans jazz did. And they are today, in their various derivative forms—popular and serious—as much a part of American and, indeed, world culture as are jazz and its many derivative musical forms and influences. This is not the place to attempt to trace the route those dance forms took up the Mississippi River to the nation at large. But it is surely there to be traced, and that difficult but important work will have to be done by historians of American dance and dance theatre.

[46]See, particularly, Berlin's "Time, Space, and the Evolution of Afro-American Society."

The African and Afro-American dances in Congo Square continued through the 1830s and 1840s. But like all other aspects of New Orleans life, the dances felt the growing American influence over the old French city. As they fell under ever-increasing scrutiny and control from municipal authorities, their regularity and frequency diminished. In 1837 the city council authorized "free negroes and slaves to give balls on the Circus Square from 12 o'clock until sunset under surveillance of the police." And in 1845 the council required that slaves at such dances have written permission from their masters and also limited the dances to two-and-a-half hours, between four and six-thirty in the afternoon, and to the four summer months of May, June, July, and August. They further required that the gathering be supervised by eight policemen and that the dances not be "offensive to public decency."[47]

[47]The unrelenting antagonism between Creoles and Americans resulted, in 1836, in the division of New Orleans into three separate municipalities, somewhat like the model offered by Paris. The government structure retained a single mayor for the whole, but each municipal council conducted its affairs as an independent city. The council referred to here is that of the First Municipality, the most decidedly Creole of the three. It ran from the river to the lake between Canal Street and Esplanade Avenue and included the French Quarter and the Faubourg Tremé. The divided city lasted until 1852 when it was reunited. See minutes of the council sittings for August 28, 1837, and April 28, 1845. The original handwritten French minutes are in the New Orleans Public Library and a somewhat incomplete printed version in French and English, "Journal of the Deliberation of the Council of the First Municipality, May 17, 1836, to May 20, 1850," in the Louisiana Collection, Tulane University Library.

Unaware of the 1837 law, Henry Kmen, "Roots of Jazz," 11ff, misinterpreted the 1845 ordinance as a restoration of dancing privileges in Congo Square. That led him and scholars who have followed him to suppose an earlier suppression and, not being able to find record of any such, to assume its existence and arbitrarily assign an 1835 date to the presumed suppression and the effective end of the dancing in Congo Square. The fact is that no such earlier suppression ordinance existed. The dances were never suspended. The word "restore" did not appear in the ordinance or in the council deliberations. It was the creation of a newspaper reporter writing a loose description of the dances for the *Daily Picayune* of June 24, 1845, and should be given no weight.

Kmen's preoccupation with the fact that the 1845 ordinance came in response to a citizens' petition asking the court to recognize the dances was also misplaced. The council commonly received such petitions and often responded with enactments. The 1845 law was actually a simple re-enactment, with slightly tigthened policing provisions, prompted by the fact that the state adopted a new constitution that year. Similar reenactments after the adoption of new constitutions were common at the levels of the state legislature, parish police juries, as well as city councils. The citizens' petititon more than likely came as a request for clarification of a series of ordinances on public dances, gambling,

In a similar vein, the council in 1839 forbade the playing of *racquettes* by slaves anywhere in the municipality. Those rough games, often played between opposing teams of Indians, whites, or blacks, began towards sundown, and drew huge unruly crowds ready for a fight. The teams alone could constitute two hundred tough players, with "the eager crowd of spectators and acquaintances running into the thousands."[48]

Aside from the disappearance of its market function and the restrictions on *racquettes* and Sunday dances, the square continued to be used as a fairground and meeting place. There were periodic circuses, fairs, horse shows, animal fights, and the like held there throughout the 1830s and 1840s. And nightime crime became an increasing problem. At various times the city fathers considered converting the square to other uses—extending Orleans Street through it and selling the lots on either side for development, offering it to the state as a site for the capitol, and erecting a municipal courthouse there—but none such came to pass.[49]

The city also periodically moved to improve the square's looks. In 1843 the council, at a cost of $1,400, removed the old

---

and public "uproar" which the council had passed during the prior few months and which, without clarification, could have been—and perhaps were being—interpreted by the police as including Congo Square's dances. See minutes of the Council's sittings for December 2, 9, 16, 19, 1844; February 17, March 3, July 15, 1845.

The real significance of the petition, which came from "citizens," not slaves, was that it represented yet another Creole attempt to preserve one of their city's cherished legacies—this time a harmless form of their beloved dancing—in the face of increasing Americanization, which became an onslaught in the 1840s. Indeed, the 1845 constitution itself represented a major watershed in the Americanization process, for under its provisions the Creoles, for the first time, lost political control of state government to the Anglos. Kmen also misread Norman, *Norman's New Orleans and Environs*, p. 182, who wrote, that the "unsophisticated" dances of the square's "primitive days," *i.e.*, the African as opposed to the Afro-American dances, had ceased, not all dances. Dena Epstein's suspicion, voiced in *Sinful Tunes*, pp. 133-135, 345, that something was wrong with Kmen's 1835 date proves to have been well founded.

[48]Council sitting on August 5, 1839. For description of the games and their crowds see Robert C. Reinders, "A Social History of New Orleans, 1850-1860" (Ph. D. dissertation, University of Texas, 1957), pp. 446-447; Castellanos, *New Orleans As It Was*, pp. 298-300.

[49]Council sittings of May 20, August 5, 1836; May 17, 1837; July 30, 1838; August 5, November 18, 1839; November 7, 1841; February 7, 1842; February 17, March 3, May 19, 1845; March 1, 1847.

wooden railings and turnstiles and surrounded *Place du Cirque* "with posts connected with iron chains, similar to that of the Washington Square," save that there would be two chains instead of one. And in 1845 they planted the square with several rows of sycamore trees set some twenty feet apart. Then in 1850-51 the council banned any more circuses in the square and had the old wrought iron fence and gates that surrounded the *Place d'Armes* taken down and reerected around Congo Square.[50] The latter move came in preparation for the refurbishment of the *Place d'Armes.* In 1850, that square, the city's central one, got a new, cast iron fence, the one still standing, and six years later, Clark Mills' famous equestrian bronze of Andrew Jackson replaced the old cannon, a war trophy from the Battle of New Orleans that had stood in the *Place* since 1815. The gun, which sounded the slave curfew at nine each evening, was also moved to Congo Square. And at the opening of 1851 the council designated the old *Place d'Armes* "Jackson Square" and simultaneously renamed Circus Square the new *Place d'Armes,* where, thenceforth, the militia drilled on Sunday afternoons.[51]

The following year, 1852, marked a turning point in New Orleans's political life, and in its cultural life as well. That year the American, i.e., English-speaking, political faction, on the rise since 1845, broke the faltering grip of the French-speaking Creole faction and took full control of municipal government. Moreover, that control slipped, within four years, into the hands of the Know-Nothings, who determined to recast the city in the image of their nativist American ideal. They proceeded more often by indirect means than by direct ones, but no less effectively. In the most notable example, they quelled

[50]Council sittings of May 17, and October 3, 16, 1843, authorized the new chain fence. Abraham O. Hall, *The Manhattaner in New Orleans: Or, Phases of "Crescent City" Life,* ed. by Henry A. Kmen (Baton Rouge, 1979), p. 106, makes it clear that the posts were wood. And he speaks of the square's "consumptive grass." See also sittings of February 3, 1845; November 11, 1850; January 13, 1851. The 1850 sitting used the phrase "Congo Square" instead of the usual "Circus Place."

[51]The First Municipal Council sittings of January 25, 1851, changed the square's name and when the city was reunified, Ordinance 660, March 15, 1853, confirmed the change. "Common Council Ordinances and Resolutions, 1852-1856." See also the *Louisiana Courier,* October 15, 1850.

and bridled the abandon with which the city had celebrated Mardi Gras since its founding, not by ordinance or police action, but by taking over the celebration, organizing it in the formal carnival "krewes" familiar today, and reshaping it along lines acceptable to Anglo-American values.[52]

The new American authorities dealt with what they regarded as the Congo Square problem by equally indirect but effective means. In 1856 the city council adopted an ordinance making it unlawful to beat a drum, blow a horn, or sound a trumpet in the city and proscribing public "immorality" and "indecency." Then followed another ordinance prohibiting all public balls, dances, and entertainments without permission from the mayor. And at the same time, the municipal gardener included in his city-beautification plan another round of tree planting for the square. The Sunday dancers, intimidated by the presence of the militia, harassed by the police, and hampered by what had become a veritable forest of saplings, came in fewer and fewer numbers after 1856, and before the end of the decade, ceased to come at all. Thus the dancing in Congo Square did not end precipitously, as some writers have supposed, but gradually, crowded out by the physical growth and the Americanization of New Orleans.[53]

So it was that on the eve of the Civil War, dancing disappeared from Congo Square. That is to say, the dancing ended as a

[52]In 1852 the city's three independent municipalities were reunited in a single city government which the Anglo faction dominated. See above, note 47. There is no full-scale history of Mardi Gras. Michael L. Osborne, *Mardi Gras: A Celebration* (New Orleans, 1981), takes note of more of its aspects than most other works.

[53]New Orleans City Council Ordinances, 1856, book 11, no. 3121 O.S., Art. 1, sec. 7, 9, 11; no. 3131 O.S.; *Daily Picayune*, March 5, 1856. The restrictive city ordinances were complemented, during the same decade, by even more repressive state enactments. For examples of the more important measures see Louisiana legislative acts 27 and 326 of 1852; act 308 of 1855; and act 187 of 1857. Severely increased restrictions on free people of color had begun in the early 1840s. See, for example, council sittings for October 31, 1842, and May 22, 1843. Fredrika Bremer's January 20, 1852, letter from New Orleans cited by Epstein, *Sinful Tunes*, p. 43, in which she complained that though she had searched for it, she found none of the famed dancing in New Orleans, tells us nothing about the demise of dancing. She was in the city in the middle of the winter, and Congo Square dancing had been restricted to the summer months since 1845. See above note 47, for the most serious misunderstanding about when and how the dancing in Congo Square ended.

public institution. But that does not mean that such dancing disappeared altogether. It continued for another thirty years or more, but with ever-diminishing frequency, and only in private settings in the city and on isolated plantations. As late as 1880 or 1881 Lafcadio Hearn saw, in a woodyard on Dumaine Street, two men beating bones and sticks on drums made from "a dry goods box and an old pork barrel" while "some old men and women" chanted an African song, and "a few old persons" with tin rattles on their ankles did African dances that, as Hearn pointed out, only they, the old ones, knew how to perform. And, Hearn added, the remnants of such dances, already rare, would soon be "completely forgotten in Louisiana."[54]

The Civil War hence marked the beginning of Congo Square's third and dismal phase. Though public Sunday dances seem to have started again after the United States Army occupied New Orleans in 1862, the revival was brief and frail. In December of 1864 the *Daily Picayune* reported that though the gates of the "pretty . . . cleanly and inviting" square "are open to admit visitors, still they do not come, at any rate they do not come like they used to. The old gun is gone, too . . . ." And by the 1870s dancing in the square was always spoken of in the past tense.[55]

In the 1870s and early 1880s, the square fell into disuse and decay, its uncut grass and unpruned sycamores as seedy and ragged as its immediate neighborhood, which became an asylum for poor Italian immigrants who began to flood into the city. In the general sprucing up the city did for the 1884-1885 Cotton Exposition, the square received some passing attention. The city gardener's crew trimmed the sycamores, removed the dead and diseased ones, planted new ones in their place, whitewashed their trunks, cut the grass, gravelled the walks, put

[54]"The Scenes of Cable's Romances," 47. See also his letter to Henry Krehbiel in Elizabeth Bisland, ed., *The Life and Letters of Lafcadio Hearn*, 2 vols. (Boston, 1906), I, 359; Henry W. Krehbiel, *Afro-American Folk Songs: A Study in Racial and National Music* (New York, 1914), p. 38; and the long quotation from a "correspondent of the *New York World*" in Herbert Asbury, *The French Quarter: An Informal History of New Orleans* (New York, 1936), pp. 252-253. Kmen identified Hearn as the correspondent.

[55]*Daily Picayune*, December 11, 1864. The federal occupation military authorities removed the cannon in 1862, and it disappeared from history.

in new park benches, took down the fence, and built a fountain in the center of the square, which was reserved for white use only.[56]

But when the Cotton Exposition ended, so did care for the now-aging square. The four decades between the late 1880s and the late 1920s represented its nadir. Unkempt and crime-ridden, it became a no man's land. The death of old Confederate General P. G. T. Beauregard in 1893 presented the city an opportunity once again to try to upgrade the old square. The authorities cut down the near-dead sycamores, replaced them with oaks, redesigned and laid new concrete walkways, planted shrubs and flower beds, and renamed their creation Beauregard Square. In 1895 they also demolished the old prison, and in 1905 built a public school for white children, McDonough 18, on St. Ann Street, facing the new square, which was reserved for white use only.[57]

But whatever benefits the neighborhood derived from those improvements were almost immediately offset by two other developments. In the late 1890s the Southern Railroad reached New Orleans and began laying its entrance tracks along the edge of the Carondelet Canal. By 1908 the tracks had reached the turning basin where they curved around a complex of freight warehouses and continued up Basin Street, through a series of huge, ugly, sheet-metal sheds built over the tracks, to an elegant passenger terminal on Canal Street. Moreover, in 1897, in an

[56]James S. Zacharie, *New Orleans Guide, With Descriptions of the Routes to New Orleans, Sights of the City Arranged Alphabetically. . . .* (New Orleans, 1885), pp. 111-112; *Historical Sketch Book and Guide*, pp. 297-298. There are a few photographs of the square, and more of the Carondelet Canal which often show the square in the background, in the collections of the University of New Orleans Archives Division, the Louisiana Collection of Tulane University Library, the New Orleans Museum of Art, the State Museum Library, and the Historic New Orleans Collection. One from the latter collection, labeled "No. 117 View in Congo Square," shows the forested square in 1884-1885. The Sanborn Fire Insurance Maps are important for the square's history after 1885. They show, among other things, the actual layout of the square after refurbishment and some of the changes in the neighborhood. The U. S. censuses reveal the influx of Italian immigrants, which lasted about thirty years, between 1890 and 1920, after which time the seven to five white-black ratio that had prevailed in Tremé since 1850 began to change as the neighborhood increasingly became black.

[57]Minutes of the New Orleans City Council for the sitting of March 28, 1893; *Daily Picayune*, March 24, 29, 1893.

effort to exercise some control on prostitution, which ran rampant in the city, the authorities designated several blocks along Basin Street, almost adjacent to Beauregard Square, as New Orleans's official red-light district, the famous Storyville, which lasted, legally, for the next twenty years.[58]

Only in the late 1920s did an upswing of sorts begin for Congo Square. The old Carondelet Canal, less and less used after the Southern Railroad began operation, silted up and became a stagnant, stinking, mosquito haven. In 1927 the city engineers condemned it as no longer navigable, filled it, and laid Lafitte Street on top of it. The 1920s also saw city authorities struggling to clean out the slum remnants of the Storyville redlight district, which, under pressure from the secretary of the United States Navy, had been deprived of its legal status in 1917. Planners conceived the idea of developing a municipal cultural complex covering several blocks around Beauregard Square to upgrade the neighborhood, which was rapidly becoming derelict and black. And they put the first segment of the complex in place in 1929-30 with the construction of the huge, multi-purpose Municipal Auditorium fronting the again refurbished, or better said, cleaned-up, square.[59]

But that was as far as the project got, at least for the next twenty-five years. During the early 1930s the Great Depression undermined city finances, which then crashed into near bankruptcy in the mid-thirties when Huey Long, acting through his rubber-stamp state legislature, stripped the city's government of virtually all administrative and financial power.

The stringent economy measures imposed by Mayor Robert S. Maestri after 1936, in his efforts to restore city finances, kept building and public-improvement programs at a standstill. Barely had he got finances on a firm footing again when World War II broke out. War shortages forced the building standstill to continue, though the war economy produced huge surpluses in the city treasury.

[58]Al Rose, *Storyville, New Orleans: Being an Authentic, Illustrated Account of the Notorious Red-Light District* (University, Ala., 1979). The Archives Division of the University of New Orleans Library has an extensive collection of photographic plates of Storyville's famous madams and their girls.

[59]Toledano and Christovich, *Faubourg Tremé*, pp. 65-66.

DeLesseps S. "Chep" Morrison, who became mayor in 1946, launched the city into a massive building program, using the wartime revenue surpluses to pay for much of it. But for nearly a decade his program focused on modernization and expansion of the city's infrastructure—utilities, drainage, streets, overpasses, and relocation of railroad tracks in order to centralize passenger traffic in a single terminal. Less basic public improvements generally had to wait.[60]

Not until 1955 did the city actually begin setting aside monies to be used for the acquisition of four city blocks surrounding Beauregard Square as called for in the old 1920s plan for construction of a cultural complex. Even so, allocations remained so small and irregular that by 1960 the fund comprised less than two million dollars. At that point the city got a windfall in the form of federal urban renewal funds, a windfall that the City Planning Commission quickly turned into a whirlwind. With the new monies the city purchased not four blocks but almost nine blocks of what had been, 150 years before, a portion of the old City Commons beyond Rampart Street. They right away moved the mostly black residents out, tore down all the ancient buildings except four, bulldozed the wells, cisterns, stables, trees, streets, and curbs, leveled the whole area, and then abandoned it for nearly ten years.[61]

Finally in 1971, after eight years of negotiations, the city began construction of a Theatre for Performing Arts in the middle of the cleared area. The death, in the same year, of the famous New Orleans jazz figure, Louis "Sachmo" Armstrong, furnished a focus for the long-open question of what to do with the urban desert the planners had created. The city immediately commissioned the San Francisco firm of Laurence Halprin and Associates, on a three-month contract, to draw up a plan for making the wasteland into a park.

After another three years of delay, and controversy over the design, the city authorized $8,200,000 to supplement a federal

[60]Entries on New Orleans mayors for the period in the Glenn R. Conrad, ed., *Dictionary of Louisiana Biography*, 2 vols. (New Orleans, 1988); and in Melvin G. Holli and Peter d'A. Jones, eds., *Biographical Dictionary of American Mayors, 1820-1980* (Westport, Conn., 1981), offer readers a convenient guide to the major literature.

[61]Toledano and Christovich, *Faubourg Marigny*, pp. 66-68; New Orleans *Times-Picayune* and the *States-Item* for the period.

grant for turning the thirty-one-acre tract into the Louis Armstrong Park. A high steel fence, made in imitation of old New Orleans wrought iron, enclosed the new park and extended around Beauregard Square, joining it to the complex. The park, with ample parking lots well disguised by careful planting, had a network of paths connecting sitting and picnic areas, and featured a sizeable lagoon, an impressive fountain system, and a series of earthen mounds, called berms, designed and placed so as to break the monotony of the naturally flat terrain.[62]

But in spite of its basically sound design, the park has proved only a limited success. Save for a few pedestrians crossing it on their way to evening performances in the theatre, it has few visitors. Two factors have militated against Armstrong Park. First, the success of the city fathers and private investors in developing the New Orleans riverfront into a competing park, with a spectacular view of the Mississippi, a world-class aquarium, and plentiful food, beverage, and shopping facilities either on the riverfront or immediately adjacent to it, has drawn most potential park users, local and tourist alike, to that location. Moreover, the land-use pattern of the French Quarter itself effectively isolates Armstrong Park. While the riverfront side of the Quarter has grown increasingly commercial and public-use oriented, the Rampart Street side has become increasingly residential. That area's quiet, almost deserted, streets offer little to attract walkers in the direction of Louis Armstrong's memorial. And the few who do make the trek find neither in or near the park any attractive shops, cafes, restaurants, or even bars, nothing, in short, to entertain them.[63]

[62]*Ibid.* A team of University of New Orleans archaeologists did some excavations in Congo Square in 1977-1978 as a condition for the federal grant. They uncovered some of the foundations of Fort St. Ferdinand, some shoring timbers from its moat and from one of the bridges that once spanned it, in addition to a number of eigtheenth-century knives, clay pipes, wine bottles, bone and wood buttons, mini balls, a 1760 Spanish coin, and numerous animal bones and teeth. Richard Shenkel, *et al., Archaeology of the Jazz Complex and Beauregard (Congo) Square, Louis Armstrong Park* (New Orleans, 1980).

[63]On similar and associated problems facing the Quarter, see "The Future of the Quarter," an unpublished 1985 report done for the Vieux Carré Commission by the Future of the Quarter Committee, Jerah Johnson, chairman. Copies on file in the Commission office and in the archives of the Earl K. Long Library at the University of New Orleans.

Aware of the problem, Mayor Sidney J. Barthelemy's administration has recently entered negotiations with the directors of Denmark's century-and-a-half old and highly successful Tivoli amusement park in Copenhagen in hopes of interesting them in adding to Armstrong Park an amusement component and food, drink, and shopping facilities needed to attract more patrons. The proposal, however, has met fierce criticism and resistence from some New Orleans groups who fear that such development may overpower or obscure the site's identity as the center of much of the city's black culture.

Whatever the solution to the problem may be, the Armstrong Park-Congo Square complex does still reflect today, in unexpected ways, a good deal of the rich history of its site. Its four remaining old buildings, to which a fifth, brought in from another part of the Faubourg Tremé, has been added, are fitted out to house a jazz museum and concert hall, and from time to time musicians and dancers give performances on the grassy field outside. The city's resident opera and ballet companies stage their productions in the Theatre for Performing Arts, and most major carnival parades still end at Congo Square, as they did in antebellum times. There the float "krewes" empty their reserves of Mardi Gras beads upon the thousand or more Tremé residents who regularly gather to be showered with the tawdry treasure. The Municipal Auditorium, which in 1946 became the first public facility in the South to be racially integrated, hosts scores of black high-school graduations each spring, most major Mardi Gras balls each winter, each summer an animal show or two, and each fall, a traveling circus.[64]

And a few aged black women—ghosts, as it were, of their distant ancestors, the slave vendors—still haunt the fringes of Armstrong Park, selling pralines and sweet potato bread to the few tourists. And, by stretching the imagination, one can even think of the berms as reminders of the long, low earthen breastwork mound that once ran along the old ramparts which separated New Orleans from its Congo Plain.

[64]The *Louisiana Courier*, February 23, 1846, described a Mardi Gras parade of that year, its long route through the city, and Congo Square as its termination point. The 1946 integration of the City Auditorium proved strictly temporary. See Katherine Ann Martensen, "Region, Religion and Social Action: The Catholic Community of the South, 1939-1956" (M.A. thesis, University of New Orleans, 1978), pp. 48ff.

Errata and Addenda

1. Text at footnote 31, erratum: Thanks to the research of Arthur Scully, Jr. of New Orleans, we now know that Signore Gaetano (Cayetano), whose surname was Mariatini (Mariotini), died in New Orleans, aged "thirty-six or thirty-seven," and was buried in St. Louis Cathedral Cemetery I on November 3, 1817. (Cathedral Interments Book 1815-1820, p. 88b, act no. 897.) And the Orleans Parish Probate Records, vol. M, 1805-1818, indicate that following his death, Mariatini's widow immediately sold off the circus horses, costumes, and equipage. Hence, his circus could not have set up in Congo Square "for a number of years" after 1816 as the text says. It is more probable that it was setting up there before 1816. The circus also likely had no wild animals. Mr. Scully is continuing research on Mariatini and his Congo Circus, also sometimes called the Olympic Circus.

2. Text at footnote 44, erratum: Thanks to the work of Reid Mitchel, "Where was Pierre Clement de Laussat during Carnival 1808?," *Louisiana History* (Winter 1993), 107, it is now clear that the dances Laussat was describing took place not in New Orleans but on the island of Martinique, where Laussat was resident prefect at the time.

3. Addendum: Nothing in the text is meant to say or imply that Congo Square was the only place in New Orleans where black New Orleanians danced. The minutes of the city council and the messages of the mayor to the council as well as travelers' accounts and various other sources from the period make it clear that, lawfully or unlawfully, slaves and free people of color held dances, privately and publicly, from time to time at any number of other locations in the city. The point here is that Congo Square was the major location where such dancing remained legal and continuous for an astonishingly long time. Similarly, to say continuous is not to say that from time to time a Sunday dance or even a season of dances was not canceled for one reason or another. But over the long haul, the practice was continuous, just as celebration of Mardi Gras in the city has been continuous, though, from time to time because of wars or police strikes or the like, it too has been temporarily suspended. (Such other locations included public dance halls where masked balls and quadroon balls were held. See R. Randall Couch, "The Public Masked Balls of Antebellum New Orleans ...," *Louisiana History* (Fall 1994), 403-431).